A Sensory History of
Ancient Warfare

First published in Great Britain in 2021 by
Pen & Sword Military
An imprint of
Pen & Sword Books Ltd
Yorkshire – Philadelphia

ISBN 978 1 47389 512 6

Typeset by Mac Style
Printed and bound in the UK by CPI Group (UK) Ltd,
Croydon, CR0 4YY.

Pen & Sword Books Limited incorporates the imprints of Atlas,
Archaeology, Aviation, Discovery, Family History, Fiction, History,
Maritime, Military, Military Classics, Politics, Select, Transport,
True Crime, Air World, Frontline Publishing, Leo Cooper, Remember
When, Seaforth Publishing, The Praetorian Press, Wharncliffe
Local History, Wharncliffe Transport, Wharncliffe True Crime
and White Owl.

For a complete list of Pen & Sword titles please contact

PEN & SWORD BOOKS LIMITED
47 Church Street, Barnsley, South Yorkshire, S70 2AS, England
E-mail: enquiries@pen-and-sword.co.uk
Website: www.pen-and-sword.co.uk

Or

PEN AND SWORD BOOKS
1950 Lawrence Rd, Havertown, PA 19083, USA
E-mail: Uspen-and-sword@casematepublishers.com
Website: www.penandswordbooks.com

A Sensory History of Ancient Warfare

Reconstructing the Physical Experience of War in the Classical World

Conor Whately

Pen & Sword
MILITARY

Contents

Acknowledgements

As is often the case, this book has been a long time coming. The initial proposal was sent off to Philip Sidnell at Pen & Sword in the winter of 2016, when I was off on my first research leave. In fact, I was fortunate enough to travel to Dubai that February with the family to visit my parents (who had lived in the Middle East for years) along with my sister and her family. While there, I vividly remember exchanging emails with Phil about the proposed book, and he suggested I shift from a focus more narrowly on the senses and war during the reign of Justinian to the ancient Mediterranean world more generally. He did ask if I'd be up for it, and I said yes, confident I could finish it all within a couple of years. My second daughter Penny was born the summer after (2017), the summer after I unexpectedly got a SSHRC IDG (Social Sciences and Humanities Research Council of Canada Insight Development Grant). These and other things, but mainly two young daughters and no family/support for thousands of miles, slowed things down to my, and Phil's, chagrin. Nevertheless, I'm thrilled that it's finally finished, albeit in a reduced and altered form.

Although I discuss Mark Smith's work as the impetus for this little book in the introduction, the person responsible for bringing this book to my attention and so planting the seed is Jonathan Eaton. Jonathan referred to Smith's *The Smell of Battle, Taste of Siege*, in a tweet, possibly in 2015 (I couldn't find the tweet), and he asked whether something similar could ever be done about the ancient world given the source limitations – we don't have the same bodies of evidence to work with that Smith did for the US Civil War. Importantly too, the timing was good: my first two books, *Battles and Generals* on Procopius, and *Exercitus Moesiae* on Roman Moesia, were done, and I was on research leave. I was also summarily unimpressed with what I had been doing and with how a great deal of the stuff I had worked on had been received. Smith's book and Jonathan's comments sparked my curiosity and gave me something else, exciting and new, to think about beyond Procopius and other matters.

Before I dish out more thanks, a note. This book is NOT meant to be authoritative or complete in its coverage; rather, I hope it offers some suggestions as to how we might approach sensory histories of war (and related issues) in the future. But more importantly, I want this book to be enjoyable to a broader audience. For a few years now, I've been eager to get my research out to the public, and I've been inspired by a wide and diverse array of scholars who have been doing this by means of books, articles, and social media, like Mary Beard, Sarah Bond, and for the Roman military, Jo Ball. I hope this will be the second (the first being my introduction to the Roman Military published by Wiley) of many such endeavours in the future.

First, a big thanks to Phil Sidnell for agreeing to publish this book and for his invaluable feedback on the manuscript. A great deal of thanks is due to the wonderful students at the University of Winnipeg who were exposed to this material in some way or another over the past four years. Some of the material in this book formed part of select lectures I gave in my Roman Arabia class in the winter of 2020, just before everything went virtual due to Covid-19. Although that class was, as its name implies, ostensibly about Arabia (Jordan and Israel/ Palestine in particular), I did devote a fair bit of time to the wider Roman Middle East, including the Jewish Wars, and so the sacks of Jerusalem and Masada. So, thanks are due to my students in that class (and many others) who contributed in one way or another to my thinking. I taught a course on Hannibal and the Punic Wars in the fall of 2017, and we spent a good amount of time on Cannae. Some of that material formed an important part of the presentation which, in turn, was the core part of the Cannae chapter. Even the last iteration of second year Greek played a part. In the first term (of the 2018–2019 year), besides little bits of grammar here and there, we read a sizeable chunk of Xenophon's *Anabasis*, and the two students, Jazz Demetrioff and Ari Haalbloom, asked what sorts of things the Greek soldiers might have eaten when off on campaign as Xenophon's were.

Three of the chapters were presented in abridged form as research papers. I presented much of the Battle of Cannae at the annual meeting of the Classical Association of Canada in 2018 in Calgary. The Battle of Issus material was presented (in part) at the annual meeting of the Classical Association of Canada in 2019 in Hamilton (McMaster). Additionally, the Strasbourg material was presented at the fall 2018 North Great Plains History Conference in Mankato (Minnesota). In that instance, I thank Graham Wrightson for the initial invitation (and discussion during the talk), and Jeff Rop, for the conversation (and introduction to deep fried cheese curds) in the interim.

As always, my family deserves special credit just for being themselves. The book was finished during the year that never ends, 2020. It's been a struggle, for all sorts of reasons: the work was unending and relentless, and trying to manage it all while everyone was home proved difficult. My wife (Hannah) and I traded on and off certain responsibilities, and somehow managed to make it to the new academic year. She (unexpectedly) has two new books of her own coming out this year as well (on primary math education), for which we (the kids, Ella and Penny, dog Don, and I) are super proud and excited. I only hope my 'Waterstones' book has a fraction of the success that I'm sure her Everything Math books will have.

I want to finish by acknowledging all the ways my wonderful colleagues at the University of Winnipeg over the years (this is my twelfth year) have contributed to this book. Jane Cahill, Matt Gibbs, Mark Golden, and Pauline Ripat welcomed me with open arms when I arrived in the late summer of 2009. I'd got the job just as I finished my PhD at Warwick. Making the shortlist for this one-year job was a tremendous shock. Getting the call from Jane just a few days before my defence in early July was nothing short of incredible. When I arrived in Winnipeg (where I stayed with my cousin Dave, who now lives somewhere in the US) and first went to visit the campus of the University of Winnipeg, Jane and Mark warmly welcomed me at the bottom of the escalators before taking me around the corner for lunch to, fittingly, Homer's. Pauline was on parental leave that first year, but I did get to meet her at a department get-together at her house. In that first and second year, I asked her so many questions about teaching (and Winnipeg) things. She's helped me in innumerable ways, and the insight into teaching and how to approach Roman history proved invaluable.

I'm so grateful to Jane, my first 'boss' there, for giving me the chance to continue (a one-year job became two one-year jobs and then three). In fact, to prove my worth, I had to teach the very myth class she'd done for so many years beforehand and have her evaluate me. Mark Golden did the same for Greek Society. In Jane's case, I used a little dose of celebrity and Lucian's *Dialogues of the Dead* to win her over. In Mark's case, interestingly enough, it was Herodotus' gold-digging ants. Jane's fabulous little book, *Her Story*, helped illuminate me to the perspectives of those often pushed to the sidelines. Amongst many other things (sports, scholarship, and more), Mark was kind enough to give me an enormous pile of old journal articles when he retired. It was a few years later, when I turned to writing the Greek chapters of this book, that I realized that they were mostly concerned with Greek war and warfare and that they were sometimes filled with his own notes.

There have been a few other colleagues who have passed through in the interim. Allison Surtees opened my eyes to aspects of satyrs, power dynamics, and Greek art, while Matt Maher gave me all sorts of valuable insight into Greek fortifications. Some wonderful colleagues moved on, like Tyson Sukava, who provided wonderful conversation over pints, and answered some unusual questions over the years on issues concerning ancient medicine. Matt Gibbs, now in Edmonton, became one of my closest friends, and really I don't think I could set out all the ways he's helped me over the years, all thanks to that night on a Winnipeg rooftop.

In the past few years, the core of the department has shifted. Pauline's still there (I'll get back to her in a moment), but we're now joined by Michael MacKinnon, Peter Miller, Melissa Funke, Vicky Austen, Chris Lougheed, and Warren Huard. Vicky's opened my eyes to the world of Columella, Roman gardens, and the occasional joys of jogging (she runs, I jog) in Winnipeg. Chris was my Covid-reading companion, as we worked our way through a number of pieces of late antique scholarship. Warren has been a faithful participant to the Friday-afternoon club (along with Carla Manfredi and Alyson

Brickey, among others, who are in the English department), and some interesting insight to Herakles and Archaic Greece. Peter Miller, our current department chair, has supported my work in a number of ways, though largely as a member of the 'beer texting group'. Melissa Funke is my across-the-hall neighbour, and I've benefitted enormously through conversations about music and Greek theatre. Michael MacKinnon has shared his vast knowledge of zooarchaeology, and all the things the Greeks and Romans ate and drank.

That note leads me to my last point. Most members of the department have some interest in the sensory experiences of the ancient Mediterranean world, and I've been lucky to discuss aspects of this work with all of them, in some capacity or other, both those who participated in our Winnipeg panel at McMaster, Melissa, Pauline, Matt, and myself, as well as Peter and Michael who didn't participate. Truly, I've been extremely lucky to have such a wonderful group of colleagues and friends, and I'd like to think they've each left their mark on this work in some way. So, with that I dedicate this book to my colleagues at the University of Winnipeg, past, present, and future.

List of Illustrations

1. Epitaph of Marcus Caelius, victim of the Battle of the Teutoburg Forest. (*Copyright Agnete, Wikimedia Commons*)
2. Achaemenid Persian Fort, Tall-e Takht, Pasargadae, Iran. The Persians had an extensive fortification network which includes sites like this, part of the Pasargadae World Heritage Site. (*Diego Delso, Wikimedia Commons*)
3. The Battle of Cunaxa fought between the Persians and 10,000 Greek mercenaries of Cyrus the Young, 401 BCE, Adrien Guiget, Louvre. (*Copyright Wikimedia Commons*)
4. Hoplite from Dodona Antikensammlung Berlin Misc. 7470. (*Copyright Wikimedia Commons*)
5. The Army of Artaxerxes II on the Tomb of Artaxerxes, Persepolis. The units (ethnic groups) depicted on the top of the frieze, from left to right, are Persian, Median, Elamite, Parthian, Arian, Bactrian, Sogdian, Choresmian, Zarangian, Arachosian, Sattagydian, Gandharan, Hindush, and haumavarga Saka. On the bottom, from left to right, are Makan, tigraxauda Saka, Babylonian, Assyrian, Arab, Egyptian, Armenian, Cappadocian, Lydian, Ionian, overseas Saka, Skudrian, Ionian with shield-hat, Libyan, Ethiopian, and Carian. (*Copyright Adobe Stock*)
6. Battle of Chaeronea, nineteenth century. (*Copyright Wikimedia Commons*)
7. The Battlefield of Issus. (*Copyright Wikimedia Commons*)
8. The location of Issus. (*Copyright Google Earth Pro*)
9. Aerial view of Issus. (*Copyright Google Earth Pro*)
10. Alexander's potential view. (*Copyright Google Earth Pro*)
11. The Alexander Mosaic, from the House of the Faun in Pompeii, Naples Archaeological Museum. (*Copyright Carole Raddato, Wikimedia Commons*)
12. Carthaginian Shekel. The Carthaginians under Hannibal famously marched across the Alps with elephants. (*Wikimedia Commons*)

Introduction

Approaching a Sensory History of Warfare in the Ancient Mediterranean World

Varus Disaster – Teutoburg Forest[1]

One of the most famous disasters in Roman history came in a forest in Germany in 9 CE. At this point, the Romans had been trying to expand their influence eastwards. In Europe, they'd been pushing towards the Elbe River with a view towards finally reaching the Vistula. For the most part, these campaigns, though not without their problems, had been going fairly well, or at least they had until Varus marched an army through the Teutoburg Forest. In this case, Varus, the governor of Germany, and about three legions (or so) had made it to the Elbe and were in the process of marching through the Teutoburg forest when they were ambushed by Arminius and his warband. Arminius, a chieftain of the Cherusci (a Germanic people), had spent a number of years serving in the Roman military as a member of the *auxilia*. As far as the Romans were concerned in 9 CE, he was still a comrade. It turned out, however, that they were horribly wrong.

While marching through some dense forest and with their guard down, thanks in part to a ruse from Arminius, the Germans struck:

> The mountains had an uneven surface broken by ravines, and the trees grew close together and very high. Hence the Romans, even before the enemy assailed them, were having a hard time of it felling trees, building roads, and bridging places that required it. They had with them many wagons and many beasts of burden as in time of peace; moreover, not a few women and children and a large retinue of servants were following them – one more reason for their advancing in scattered groups. Meanwhile a violent rain

and wind came up that separated them still further, while the ground, that had become slippery around the roots and logs, made walking very treacherous for them, and the tops of the trees kept breaking off and falling down, causing much confusion. While the Romans were in such difficulties, the barbarians suddenly surrounded them on all sides at once, coming through the densest thickets, as they were acquainted with the paths. At first they hurled their volleys from a distance; then, as no one defended himself and many were wounded, they approached closer to them. For the Romans were not proceeding in any regular order, but were mixed in helter-skelter with the wagons and the unarmed, and so, being unable to form readily anywhere in a body, and being fewer at every point than their assailants, they suffered greatly and could offer no resistance at all.[2]

But that wasn't it. Though they lost quite a few men on that night, there was still more carnage to come, with the ordeal spread over a few days:

Upon setting out from there they plunged into the woods again, where they defended themselves against their assailants, but suffered their heaviest losses while doing so. For since they had to form their lines in a narrow space, in order that the cavalry and infantry together might run down the enemy, they collided frequently with one another and with the trees. They were still advancing when the fourth day dawned, and again a heavy downpour and violent wind assailed them, preventing them from going forward and even from standing securely, and moreover depriving them of the use of their weapons. For they could not handle their bows or their javelins with any success, nor, for that matter, their shields, which were thoroughly soaked. Their opponents, on the other hand, being for the most part lightly equipped, and able to approach and retire freely, suffered less from the storm.[3]

The outcome was the same, the slaughter of Roman soldiers. The end result was the death of 10,000 to 15,000 on the Roman side, and only 500 to 1,500 on the German side.

These detailed passages come from Cassius Dio, who wrote an extensive history of Rome in the third century CE in Greek, and who describes the battle in detail, despite writing centuries later. Word did eventually reach Rome of the carnage, but it would be a few years before the Romans were able to return and make some attempt at burying the dead. In the modern era, it wasn't until fairly recently that the battlefield was found, owing to the presence of a remarkable quantity of Roman small finds.[4] Bodies were hard to come by, though this isn't surprising.[5] What we do have is the epitaph of one of its participants. In translation, from the original Latin, it reads:

> To Marcus Caelius, son of Titus, of the Lemonian district, from Bologna, first centurion of the eighteenth legion. 53½ years old. He fell in the Varian War. His freedman's bones may be interred here. Publius Caelius, son of Titus, of the Lemonian district, his brother, erected (this monument). [CIL 13.8648]

Image 1 in the plate section is of the epitaph in its entirety with both the Latin inscription and its iconographic compliment. Though only one man, and a high ranking one at that, if we pay close attention to his background and the course of battle, such as we have it, and do this while being attentive to the five traditional senses (sight, smell, sound, taste, and touch), we can get a better sense of what it was like to have lived through the battle for men like Caelius.

One of the things that stands out from what we know about the battle is how close together everyone was, a point brought out by Cassius Dio. The marching column was so tightly packed in part because of the terrain. On the one side, the narrow track was lined with trees and dense forest, and just beyond a bog. On the other, more trees, but also a not insignificant hill, Kalkriese Hill. To complicate matters further for the Romans, the Germans built a wall of sod, parts of which have been excavated, which narrowed the track and gave them additional protection from attack.[6]

Caelius, as a centurion, would have been marching with his century, which in turn was part of that eighteenth legion. It's hard to know exactly where he would have been specifically amongst the masses, though it was often the light infantry and cavalry at the vanguard and rearguard, which makes it likely that Caelius was somewhere in the middle. Ordinarily, while marching, the soldiers would be relatively well spaced, at least as the circumstances warranted. We don't know exactly how much space there was between soldiers, so it might have been no more than a few feet between soldiers in front, behind, and on either side of Caelius, unless he was positioned on the end. Though Caelius and these soldiers would have been relatively well trained, defensive manoeuvres, involving sword and shield, two of the standard pieces of equipment of the early imperial legionary, would have been limited by the amount of space. Plus, if missiles were falling from all sides, as they likely were, we can well imagine the soldiers looking one way and then another as they tried to get in position to fend off the attack. Orders would surely have come, and the Romans would have done their best, but the unexpectedness of the attack and the limited space would seem to confirm Cassius' words – the bumping into one another and the trees. This on its own would likely have thrown some soldiers off balance. Throw in the wind, rain, and debris from the trees, and not only would Caelius feel the wind and the rain on his face, depending on which day of the attack it was, but also, maybe, a log at his feet, which he might have stumbled over while shifting in position; this, if he fell over, might well have been followed by the crush of his comrades. Though he might have tried to grip his spear, sword, and shield, it was exceedingly wet and they were slippery, and so in trying to hold on to one, he might have lost grip on the others. If he fell over, as many likely did, he would soon feel the bottoms of the soldiers' feet, and possibly too bits of dirt, wood, and even the edges of Roman shields.

It seems clear, then, from the perspective of touch, that Caelius' somatosensory system might well have been overwhelmed, which is to say nothing of the responses of his other sensory systems. A constant barrage of missiles from unknown and varied locations might well have induced fear. And while Caelius might have seen much of this unfold – the missiles, the muck, the sight of his comrades rising and falling – there would have been a great deal that he didn't, like the faces and identities of his attackers. If he had had personal slaves and/or servants, he might not see them. Varus and the high command might also have been too far ahead to get noticed. Plus, if they were short on food after the previous days' attacks, Caelius might also be hungry and thirsty. The physical exertion of these attacks alone would have weakened him. So, he would have to combat all of this, hunger, thirst, the weight of his comrades, the slipperiness of his weapons, the muck of the earth, all while only seeing a little of what was going on, and while surrounded by a wall of sound composed of yelling, screaming – women and children too Cassius Dio says – in a variety of languages, the wind, the whizz of missiles, the thud of spears and arrows on shields, and the clanging of steel, and much more besides all mixed in together. A battle like this, especially a defeat like this, would have been a sensory overload for the participants like Caelius, and knowing this about the sensory experience helps us to understand why the Romans lost. It would have been difficult for anyone to maintain their position and fight on in these conditions, especially over the course of a few days.

Because he was a centurion, Caelius might have expected a little more out of life than his even-lower-ranking fellow-soldiers. Outside of this battle, he would have got more money, which we can see in the very existence of his tombstone, made after his death many miles from home. We can see it too in terms of whose remains were able to be interred on that very spot, at Xanten, where he was likely based.[7] Regardless of his age at death, Caelius had accumulated enough money to free at least one slave; moreover, on the tombstone itself, he's flanked by two slaves, possibly, if not probably, a reflection of his wealth.[8] Some of the remains from the battlefield included the wide range of utensils used by the Romans in the preparation of food, like wine strainers and buckets, all of bronze. But they also found silver spoons, the sort of thing most likely to be used by members of the officer class like Caelius.[9] The additional varied paraphernalia on the tombstone also tells us something about his career: the medals on his armour and the oak-leaf crown tell us about his military service. While centurions were meant to keep those serving under them in order, they weren't immune from rash feats of daring, as the story of Pullo and Vorenus from Caesar's Gallic Wars attests.[10] Given his past record, Caelius might well have attempted the same here at the Teutoburg Forest. His comparative wealth, however, suggests that he need not have suffered quite to the same degree as his men. If Caelius had survived the first couple of days, even without tents (lost after day one) and much more besides, he might well have had a better night's sleep than the 80 to 100 men at his command.[11] He could have expected a little more care to his material wellbeing, how he felt (how warm he was), what he ate, and what he drank.

In short, what Caelius experienced would have differed in significant ways from his peers. Using the available evidence and thinking about senses allows us to get a fuller understanding of lived experience in the ancient Mediterranean, here in combat. Moreover, it can offer more besides, on the one hand by allowing us to go beyond the generic experiences to see how dissimilar groups experienced things differently, and on the other hand by helping us make sense of what exactly transpired.

Senses and Warfare in the Ancient Mediterranean World

This book offers a short introduction to the sensory history of warfare in the ancient Mediterranean world. The five senses – sight, sound, touch, taste, and smell – have long been a feature of writing about ancient warfare. Homer's *Iliad*, the benchmark and starting point for all subsequent accounts of warfare, from the historical to the poetic, made the senses a big part of his story. The gory wounds and vivid death scenes regularly appeal to the senses of the listener or reader. To give but one example, just after the death of his comrade Leucus, Odysseus kills one of Priam's sons, Democoon, which for Homer went something like this:

For his slaying waxed Odysseus mightily wroth at heart, and strode amid the foremost warriors, harnessed in flaming bronze; close to the foe he came and took his stand, and glancing warily about him hurled with his bright spear; and back did the Trojans shrink from the warrior as he cast. Not in vain did he let fly his spear, but smote Priam's bastard son Democoon, that had come at his call from Abydus, from his stud of swift mares. Him Odysseus, wroth for his comrade's sake, smote with his spear on the temple, and out through the other temple passed the spear-point of bronze, and darkness enfolded his eyes, and he fell with a thud and upon him his armour clanged.[12]

Even the epithets that fill the pages of both the *Iliad* and *Odyssey* often consciously evoke some aspect of the sensory experience, like one of the more famous ones, 'rose-fingered Dawn'. Thucydides, the fifth century BCE Greek historian, gave a privileged position to sight in his discussion of the perils of reconstructing the famed night battle at Epipolae.[13] While reconstructing the battle during the day is difficult, when you cannot see the task it is considerably trickier.[14] In that specific context (battle), Thucydides followed other ancient thinkers in placing sight above the other four senses.[15] Only two short examples, but they illustrate an existing ancient awareness in the relationship between senses and warfare.

A focus on senses can do much more than elucidate the experience of the participants, as illuminating and engaging as this is. To give another, later, example from the end of antiquity, many have cautioned against privileging sight,[16] and indeed in antiquity too there was debate about its place in the sensory hierarchy.[17] But, as noted, sight was the predominant sense in the Classical world.[18] To use a sixth century example, Procopius' *Wars* regularly provides examples where social position affected what one saw in war, especially in the context of the honour-shame culture that pervaded most sixth century CE warriors, often with a lower social standing, as exemplified by the many 'heroic displays'.[19] While it was incumbent on leading generals like Belisarius to see these heroic displays to divvy out the appropriate awards,[20] the Emperor Justinian himself commissioned grand visual testaments to his wars, without ever seeing combat himself.[21] A focus on the senses means not just looking at how they were experienced, but what impact they had on the wider social and cultural context.[22]

Scholars and, so far as I can tell, more general authors have shied away from an emphasis particularly on the sensory experience. There has, of course, been plenty of work done on war in antiquity, from studies of individual wars and the practice of war, to, following Keegan, the face-of-battle approach to combat.[23] Some of those face-of-battle studies have delved into the experience of war, though none have looked at the full spectrum of experience (five senses), and from the perspectives of both soldiers and civilians.

The impetus for this book is another by Mark Smith entitled *The Smell of Battle, the Taste of Siege: A Sensory History of the Civil War* published in 2015 by OUP. Divided into five neat chapters, Smith covers the sounds of the assault on Fort Sumter in Charleston, the sights of First Bull Run, the smells of Gettysburg, hunger at Vicksburg, and the close-quarters of the submarine *H.L. Hunley*.[24] While Smith's book is one of the earliest ventures of sensory history into military studies, this burgeoning field has attracted considerable attention, and among scholars of the ancient Mediterranean (generally Greece, Rome, and their neighbours) too. Sensory history involves exploring how the senses have shaped experiences in the past and is a two decades-old field in history and a burgeoning field among Classicists.[25] Routledge, for instance, has a new series entitled 'the Senses in Antiquity'.

The use of modern methodologies to evaluate aspects of the ancient world is hardly unusual, and is best exemplified in the case of ancient warfare by the various 'face of battle' studies.[26] Those studies go some way towards describing the experience of ancient combat, concerned as they are with common soldiers, but they only scratch the surface. Smith's book goes further, bringing the war to life from the perspective of the five common senses; moreover, as Smith has noted elsewhere, sensory history offers significant potential for social history too.[27] Where face of battle approaches attempt to show how the experiences of the common soldiers influenced the outcome of combat, a sensory approach can look beyond battle to how its experiences reflect social issues, like power relations.

As I said, the various 'face of battle' studies have illuminated a great deal of the experiences of the common soldiers.[28] Digging deeper might seem problematic, for Smith was able to draw on a body of evidence that we do not have in antiquity, namely early photographs, newspaper reports, and personal diaries, among others. Yet, despite these seeming limitations, we have extensive accounts of warfare, and some of the striking and useful pieces of evidence include the historical epics (Homer's *Iliad*), Latin histories (Livy's *Ab Urbe Condita*), later classicizing histories (Procopius' *Wars*), and military manuals (Maurice's *Strategikon*).

Ultimately, applying a sensory approach to ancient warfare not only has the potential to elucidate the experience of ancient combat, but also to illustrate how those from different social positions participated in warfare in varied ways.

The Sources

Scholars have been drawn to sensory history in increasing numbers over the past ten to fifteen years, and a few studies have appeared that approach aspects of the ancient world using this framework. Unfortunately, we lack the same kind of evidence for war in the ancient Mediterranean: there are no diaries, journals, and newspaper articles, for instance. This is why my book will not be focussed on one sense in a particular engagement (a chapter, say, devoted to smell in the Battle of Dara). Rather, each chapter will provide something of a composite image of how the impact of all the senses on individuals, both soldiers and civilians alike, affected both their experience in, and the conduct of, war in individual ancient battles and sieges.

In the absence of the same detailed sources to work with that Smith had when looking into the US Civil War, I have to rely on a wide range of often-inconsistent and challenging materials, from narrative histories to epic poems. In subsequent chapters, I'll highlight some of the key sources for each topic. Here, rather than repeat what I'll later say, I want to draw your attention to some of the important details of the evidence we do have for ancient warfare and highlight both its strengths and its weaknesses.

I'm going to start with the most obvious category of evidence, the ancient histories. There are plenty of these. The first, written in Greek, was Herodotus' *History*, and right from the offing war took centre stage. Each chapter in this book has the benefit of one long, detailed historical narrative that provides much of the evidence. In chapter one it's Xenophon's *Anabasis*; in chapter two it's Arrian's *Anabasis*; in chapter three it's Polybius' *History* or Livy's *Ab Urbe Condita*; in chapter four it's Josephus' *Jewish War*; in chapter five it's Ammianus Marcellinus' *Res*

Gestae; and in chapter six Procopius' *Wars*. These traditional histories make war and politics their focus, so they are often full of important details. While these sorts of classical and classicizing histories are extremely valuable, they have their limitations. They tend to highlight the generals at the expense of the low-ranking soldiers.

Moving beyond the literary, we have a wealth of papyrological, legal, and material evidence that should help flesh out the sensory experience of war. The papyrological evidence, for instance, primarily from Egypt although there are also papyri from Israel/Palestine and Jordan, is devoted, in part, to foodstuffs and the trade in animals. It therefore provides some additional evidence for the sorts of foods people were likely to eat, and some of the animals they would likely have been exposed to on a regular basis. The physical evidence contributes to our understanding of the experience of warfare in manifold ways, from the diet of soldiers to their living conditions. We saw some of this above with Kalkriese. But wider considerations are important too, like local topography and the assorted weather patterns. These can all play a role in some way or other, in understanding the sensory experience. In sum, limitations aside, we have more than enough varied evidence to provide at least a cursory sensory history of warfare in the ancient Mediterranean, a topic and approach that has not yet been applied to any part of the military history of the Classical and post-Classical worlds.

The Book

Smith's book, divided into five chapters, uses each of the five senses to help understand one particular engagement. Thus, one chapter is devoted to the sounds of the Battle of Fort Sumter (April 1861), and another to the impact of the visual on our understanding of the Battle of First Bull Run (July 1861). We lack the same kind of evidence for war in the ancient Mediterranean, as we've just seen: there are no diaries, journals, and newspaper articles, for instance. As such, while I do look at individual engagements, in each chapter I cover all five senses rather than just one.

It should also be clear that this is a short book. It's not meant to be the first or last word on senses and ancient combat. It consciously mimics Smith's approach in his own work on the civil war. To that end, each of the chapters is focussed, for the most part, on an individual battle, starting at the tail end of the fifth century BCE and running up to the middle of the sixth century CE. Furthermore, the chapters are divided into three groups of two: there are two Greek chapters, two Roman chapters, and two late antique chapters. The first chapter concentrates on the Battle of Cunaxa in 401 CE. While most of the discussion focuses on that disastrous battle, at least for Cyrus and the Greeks, I also touch on aspects of the Greeks' long march home. The second chapter shifts to Alexander and the Battle of Issus in 333 BCE, and how topography impacted sight, among other things. The second part is the Roman section. Chapter 3 looks into the sensory experience of the famed Battle of Cannae between Rome and Carthage in 216 BCE. The time of year meant certain major weather patterns had an impact on the battle's course and how it would have been experienced. In the fourth chapter, I turn to the first siege of the book, the Siege of Masada (72 CE), which came near the end of the first century CE Jewish War. I also cover aspects of the Siege of Jerusalem and look at Babatha's experiences in the cave of letters during the Bar Kokhba revolt. The third section is the late antique section. Chapter 5 is on the Battle of Strasbourg in 357 CE, in which Julian's Roman army fought a much larger army of Alamanni. The sixth and final chapter returns to siege warfare. It looks at the Siege of Edessa in 544 CE, in which the Edessenes were besieged by the Sasanid Persians. Along the way, however, I touch on the similarity between the siege mounds at Edessa with our evidence for the mines and towers at Dura Europos, which have been the subject of significant attention. Besides going over some specific features of each of the six battles and sieges and some comparative material, I also provide an introduction to the sources and the wider context in each chapter.

Part I

The Greek World

Chapter 1

The Battle of Cunaxa (401 BCE)

The story begins in the eastern Mediterranean in the aftermath of the Peloponnesian War (431–404 BCE). Athens and Sparta were at peace, and a wide variety of Greek city states were allied with Achaemenid Persia. Cyrus the Younger, a pretender to the throne, enlisted many thousands of Greeks in his quest to overthrow Artaxerxes II, the then *shahanshah* (king of kings) of Persia. The two sides, the rebel Persians and their allies under Cyrus the Younger on the one hand and the imperial forces on the other, met at Cunaxa, not far from Babylon in modern day Iraq, in early September of 401 BCE (see Image 3). The outcome was a victory for the incumbents – Artaxerxes II would continue to rule until 358 BCE – and a crushing defeat for the pretender, or at least its leader, Cyrus. While, under different circumstances, this battle would have had a minimal impact on the historical consciousness of the wider western Mediterranean, among the Greeks on the losing end was Xenophon, a prolific Athenian author and commander who had a soft spot for Sparta. Xenophon and his countrymen had to march through enemy territory from Iraq back to Greece, and though they lost many men on the way, Xenophon succeeded, so living to tell the tale. This is the story of Xenophon's *Anabasis*, or *Journey Upcountry*, which includes a detailed account of that very battle.[1] While there are all sorts of things we could say about the sensory experiences of the campaign, in this opening chapter I will focus specifically on the battle at Cunaxa and the experience of combat.

Background[2]

The *Anabasis*, written in Attic Greek, is full of drama and tragedy. The Greeks, understandably, serve as the focus of the action, and Xenophon details several Greek contingents, including soldiers from

Boeotia, Achaea, Arcadia, Thessaly, and Sparta among others.[3] These soldiers were, by and large, infantry, with some 10,000 or so heavily armoured hoplites, and some 2,500 or so of the more lightly armed peltasts. In fact, Xenophon's fighting force is usually known as 'the Ten Thousand'.[4] Although Xenophon's literary artistry hasn't been at the top of anyone's list for a long time, recent readers have been paying more attention, or have at least been more aware of the skill he deftly wields.[5] For instance, an important part of Xenophon's technique is his focalization on the Greeks in this battle, which draws attention to their actions and exaggerates their importance at the expense of the rest of the participants.[6]

While Xenophon's account is the most famous description of the battle and the campaign, we also have the account of Diodorus Siculus, or Diodorus of Sicily, who wrote an encyclopaedic universal history of the world as he knew it in the first century BCE. Like Xenophon he wrote in Greek, and he included much of the same information, but also some different material, some of which is preferable to Xenophon's. For instance, both writers claim that the two armies, those of Cyrus and Artaxerxes, were massive. Xenophon, however, claims that Cyrus had an army about 200,000 strong, while Artaxerxes had one nearly 1,000,000 strong.[7] Though still large, Diodorus' figures, apparently based on the earlier source Ephorus, are a little more believable: he claims that Artaxerxes' force numbered closer to 400,000.[8] Diodorus, who relied heavily on the works of others, used Xenophon's description of the battle as the foundation for his own, and then supplemented it with some other, now lost, material, including accounts by the aforementioned Ephorus as well as Ctesias.[9] Plutarch too, for that matter, in his biography of Artaxerxes, includes the odd incidental detail, and makes explicit reference to aspects of these lost accounts.[10]

What we don't have is much in the way of explicit archaeological material specifically from this battle. There are all sorts of physical remains from Greek soldiers and even some from other battlefields. We know what sorts of things Greek soldiers wore and what they used in battle. We have visual representations of this too on the abundant iconographic evidence of Greek pottery, though much of this is a century or more earlier in date. There is often the odd statue, like the hoplite from Dodona at the Antikensammlung in Berlin (Image 4). One of the most striking artefacts from the Royal Ontario Museum in Toronto is a Corinthian Helmet complete with skull, which is said to hail from the Battle of Marathon. Even more spectacular, perhaps, are the remains of the dead from the Battle of Chaeronea, fought in 338 BCE between a Greek and Macedonian army (Image 6). That battle is often held out as the last stand of Greece – they lost. One of the most famous groups to perish in the fighting were from the Sacred Band from Thebes. A number of skeletons were buried together, and by some reckoning these were the remains of members of that group, interred after the battle.[11] The direction from which they received their wounds implies that they were attacked from above, by cavalry, which some say is purported to have happened to the Sacred Band in the battle. While this varied and assorted archaeological evidence from Greek warfare is not specific to Cunaxa, chronologically (and by ancient standards) it's not far off. It can tell us something about the experience of hoplites in battle in the Classical age.

Greek Soldiers and Warfare[12]

Hoplites were some of the most famed warriors/soldiers of the ancient Mediterranean world.[13] Traditionally, they were middle-class soldiers with agrarian backgrounds, who paid for their own equipment. Some of the most distinctive aspects of these soldiers were their heavy bronze breastplates, their concave shields (the *aspis* or *hoplon*), and their greaves. They often restricted their fighting to warmer times of year, though not always. Another distinctive feature was their helmet, which over time came in a few different shapes and sizes, with arguably the best known being the Corinthian helmet.

As noted, battle in the Classical era, from the Achaemenid Persian invasion of Greece to Philip's victory over the Greeks, was usually restricted when it came to the time of year. Most argue that Greek soldiers were amateurs, who spent a good part of the rest of their lives attending their farms. As a result of this, they could only leave their crops for so long; hence the restrictions.[14] Along the same lines, service was restricted to certain members of the population because you needed to have the requisite financial requirements to buy the necessary equipment, the purchase of which was incumbent on the individual. It also seems to have been the case that citizenship was an important requirement for would-be soldiers, especially in places like Sparta that fought hard, often brutally and ruthlessly, to restrict access to full citizen status.[15] Indeed, by many accounts, citizenship became ever more exclusive in Greece over the Classical period. Sometimes, however, desperate times could lead to exceptional circumstances. During crises, all able-bodied citizens over the age of 18 could be called upon to line up in the formed ranks of the hoplite phalanx,[16] which the evidence implies was largely a Classical era phenomenon.[17]

Besides their weapons and their armour, the hoplites were well known for the distinctive formation in which they fought, the phalanx, which was a closely packed, serried formation. Because of its reliance on infantry with little training and the vital role that the integrity of the battle line played in its effectiveness, there is good reason to suppose that, in many circumstances, battles would be sought on wide and level plains. This sort of topographic environment made the success of the phalanx all the more likely. What's more, when Greeks fought against Greeks, foes were usually fighting in similar formations, and both sought out similar locations, though some of these widely held assertions have been challenged.

The origins of the phalanx are murky. Some see it as a product of the Archaic Age in Greece (800–479 BCE) and describe the arrival of the hoplite and its use of the phalanx as a revolution in warfare.[18] More recent research, however, points towards the emergence of the phalanx and the hoplite in the Classical era, from about 479 BCE on, that is from the second Persian invasion of Greece.[19] It seems too that it wasn't until late in the fifth century BCE that the term phalanx, though dating back to Homer, started getting used regularly, with Xenophon himself a key arbiter of this change.[20] Whether changes in equipment led to the development of the phalanx or vice versa is less clear.[21]

A closer look at the hoplite and the phalanx allows us to consider in more detail the first sensory aspect of this battle: touch. The typical phalanx included lines of closely placed men, standing nearly shoulder to shoulder, with similarly arrayed men in front of them and behind them – unless they were positioned at the front or at the back. It's very likely then that if you were a hoplite standing in the middle of the formation, you might just about feel the men standing around you, though it would depend on the particular circumstances. Like many aspects of Greek warfare, there are plenty of debates about the spacing between soldiers.[22] Though, when first arrayed, there likely would have been a few feet separating one hoplite from another on all sides, if the formation was surrounded and the men hemmed in, it mightn't take long for the men to be standing literally shoulder to shoulder.

Sometimes, however, touch might play a deliberate role in how a hoplite performed. A significant part of the phalanx's effectiveness was attached to the employment of an action called the *othismos*, or shove. Its character is obscure. Some see the *othismos* as a literal shove, along the lines of the pushing of one group of rugby players against another in a scrum, others see the push of the phalanx as something metaphorical. If the *othismos* was a literal shove, then this would obviously have involved a fair amount of touching. In this scenario, the hoplite soldier would push against the back of the man in front of him, and in turn he would feel the push of his comrade behind him, with shield pushing upon back. The men at the front would push against their foes, in many scenarios an enemy phalanx, and hope to push it back. If this happened, it could lead to the opposing men breaking up their own formation and so leaving them more susceptible to enemy attack. If those being pushed on the other side also lost their balance, they might conceivably stumble back into each other, so causing them to bunch up. In this case they would feel the physical weight of their fellow-soldiers.[23] All that said, serious doubts have been raised about this push or shove, and so we shouldn't put too much faith in it occurring in this battle, or any for that matter.

Hoplites weren't the only types of troops who fought in Classical Greece, even if they were the most famous. There were also archers, cavalry, and light infantry, though they weren't as prestigious and, depending on the place, not used as often. In Athens, the hoplite was more prestigious than the cavalry, a reflection of who served as hoplites. That said, hoplites were also the least professional of soldiers, amateurs, unlike, by comparison, the members of the Athenian navy. For some

Greeks like Xenophon, all the hoplites needed to perform well was their bravery and fitness. Given their amateur status and particular approach to combat, hoplites often had to rely on the support of those other troops, especially the light infantry and the cavalry, who were themselves instrumental in the most destructive phase of battle, the rout.[24]

Cunaxa

As you might expect in the description of a battle in which the author, Xenophon, played a role, his account is not without its problems. For one thing, his account has made it seem that the Greek allied hoplites, the so-called mercenaries, were the only soldiers on Cyrus' side that fared well against Artaxerxes II's forces (see Image 5 for a contemporary representation of Artaxerxes' army). In this narrative, they evinced the superiority of Western over Eastern armies, a fact evident decades earlier during the two failed Persian invasions of mainland Greece. But this view puts too much weight on the supposed East-West dichotomy, when in reality the Greeks were a much smaller power when compared to the Achaemenid behemoth, who faced problems at different times on multiple fronts.

The Greek soldiers who fought for Cyrus are usually characterized by modern scholars as mercenaries, but Rop has recently made a forceful argument that we should see them fighting for Persia less out of a need for money, and more because of their patronage responsibilities.[25] Greeks fought for Persia because of the series of alliances forged in the fifth and fourth centuries BCE; they continued to serve through the course of the fourth century BCE.

To get back to the point raised in the previous paragraph, it wasn't that the Greeks were better than the Persians, which was why they wanted them there in first place. Rather, the Greek infantry could fill a need in the Persian rebel army. Indeed, hoplites in a tightly organized phalanx could perform quite well in combat against charging cavalry, an arm of the Persian military for which they were famous. Persian chariots and cataphracts were noteworthy, but hoplites in a phalanx weren't unbreakable against charging Persians, especially against well trained and carefully organized Persian cavalry.

The Sounds of Cunaxa

So what do we find at Cunaxa? For one thing, the Persian army under Artaxerxes II was a sight to behold:

> Midday came and still there was no sign of the enemy, but early in the afternoon a cloud of dust appeared, looking at first like a white cloud in the sky. Some time later, however, it was as if there was a huge black smudge on the plain. Before long, as the enemy drew nearer, there were flashes of bronze, and then the tips of their spears and the divisions of the enemy army became apparent. On the left wing there were cavalrymen in white cuirasses, reported to be under the command of Tissaphernes; next to them were foot soldiers with wicker shields and then heavily armed troops, rumoured to be from Egypt, with wooden shields which reached down to their feet. Then there were further cavalry units and more archers. All of them marched in serried squares, with a different people making up each square. In front of them, and at some distance from one another, were the scythe-bearing chariots, as they are called; they were equipped with scythes which projected out sideways from their axles and faced the ground under the chariots as well, so as to cut to pieces anything or anyone they met. The plan was to use these chariots against the Greeks as they advanced in formation to break up the enemy lines. But one thing Cyrus said at the meeting he had convened turned out to be wrong: he had urged the Greeks to stand firm against the barbarians' clamour, but in actual fact they made no noise, but advanced slowly and steadily, in all possible silence.[26]

This vivid description captures well the possible Greek reaction to the arrival of the massive Persian army. Xenophon uses sight and sound to convey some of the potential fear felt by those Greek soldiers. But for all there was to see at Cunaxa, there was also plenty to hear. Some are more generic, for there are all sorts of other sounds usually associated with the start of a battle involving a phalanx in Classical Greece.

For one thing, there's a lot of uncertainty in the description about the character of the Persian contingents, with all the information seemingly passed by rumour, that is by sound – word of mouth. Although he doesn't elaborate, and even taking the tendencies of historians like Xenophon into consideration, it seems likely that this information could have been passed by word of mouth from one man to another. On the other hand, at the end of the passage it's not so much the noise that the army makes that warrants it getting singled out, as the noise it doesn't make – the silence as they advanced into battle.

The Persian silence as they advanced towards battle contrasts sharply with the noise coming from the Greek side. This is due, in part, to the perspective provided by Xenophon, who seems to have been up front and in a position to hear it all. For one thing, Xenophon's description makes it clear that the Persian army was a polyglot one, with contingents from a variety of places. As soon as he turns to Cyrus' army, he notes the would-be king rode along the line with his translator, Pigres, while he shouted orders to Clearchus, who was in charge of the Greek contingent, and the others. This action is standard fare in ancient combat. Commanders and generals regularly rode among their ranks at the front of their armies giving instructions. Sometimes historians like Xenophon present these as long, detailed speeches, given just before the battle begins. In turn, the opposing commander usually gives a speech of his own that might respond to his foes' comments. It's unlikely that speeches were ever given before battle quite like this – the specific situation that Xenophon describes before Cunaxa is far more likely.[27] For one thing, sometimes opposing commanders spoke different languages, which makes understanding their opponent's words difficult if not impossible depending on the circumstances. For another thing, the number of participants in a given battle might be large, which would make it physically impossible to convey the words a commander spoke to all the participants. This is why, as I say, a scenario like this, where the commander, here Cyrus, rides along the ranks shouting out commands to other commanders, is far more probable.

From the shouting of Cyrus and his translator, Xenophon shifts to some quieter and more personal chitchat of Xenophon and Cyrus. There was likely plenty of idle – and otherwise – conversation in the moments leading up to first contact (and in the course of battle too). But sound is also used to play up the excitement of what's enfolding. After Cyrus had given some instructions to Xenophon, he heard something else, and asked the Athenian what it was. Xenophon replied that it was the watchword passed through the lines. Cyrus' unfamiliarity with this apparent Greek practice reveals something of the difficulty in communications in combat, but also some of the unfamiliarity between contingents in the army, a possible red flag for future problems. In Classical-era Greek combat, a key part in communications in the build-up to the clash of the two sides was the salpinx, which looked a bit like a trumpet, and which was used to indicate that the soldiers should charge or retreat. As the battle started to intensify, however, it became more difficult to pass instructions. Xenophon himself, in a different context, says, 'there was no shouting, nor was there silence, but the strange noise that wrath and battle together will produce'.[28] Shouting was a common practice, but it had limited use, so to get new instructions passed down the line, the Greeks might use watchwords passed along like here at Cunaxa.[29] In some cases, messengers on horseback could relay commands to other contingents in an army, as happened at Plataea.[30]

But let's get back to that Persian silence. As significant as it seems to have been to Cyrus' side, it contrasts quite sharply with the Greeks' own practice. When the two armies were ready to advance, the Greeks struck up the paean and began to advance against their foes. The paean was a hymn sung by many Greeks as they marched into battle (and sometimes afterwards), often used to ward off evil. Some, like the Spartans, preferred to sing something else, a hymn to Castor according to Plutarch.[31] There's also likely to have been the sounding of a trumpet (*salpinx*) to signal the advance, as I noted above.[32] That wasn't it for the sounds the Greeks emitted at this battle. Xenophon tells us that, as their phalanx (they were mostly infantry hoplites) surged forward and broke into a run, all the soldiers yelled out a war-cry to Enyalius, a god of war sometimes considered an alternative name for Ares.[33] And, as Xenophon has it, they clashed their spears against their shields as they advanced to intimidate the Persians further.[34]

Another key feature was the war cry, and it seemed that just about every different people in the ancient Mediterranean had their own war cry, some of which were quite distinctive.[35] The sheer number of Persian soldiers at Cunaxa meant that their cry was particularly loud. Xenophon said, 'The enemy army is vast and as they advance they will raise a terrific clamour'.[36] The Greeks too had distinctive war cries, and this varied, in some cases, from place to place. Besides the aforementioned paeans sung by many, some also cried out to Ares, the god of war.[37] The Spartans, on the other hand, seemed to have been fond of the poetry of Tyrtaeus, one of our most important sources for Archaic Greek combat.[38] Plutarch gives a detailed account of the Spartans' musicality, stressing they were noted both for this and their warlike spirit.[39] Whether the songs he records were themselves sung before battle isn't entirely clear. Nevertheless, he does give the following evocative description:

> the king…ordered the pipers to pipe the strains of the hymn to Castor; then he himself led off in a marching paean, and it was a sight equally grand and terrifying when they marched in step with the rhythm of the flute, without any gap in their line of battle, and with no confusion in their souls, but calmly and cheerfully moving with the strains of their hymn into the deadly fight.[40]

In short, these cries and others like them were distinctive features of Greek battle cries.

The Sights of Cunaxa

Although, so far, I've been highlighting mostly the sounds of the battle, it's worth drawing attention to some of the sights too, which I only hinted at earlier. Greek soldiers might go to extraordinary lengths to emphasize their appearance in battle. If Plutarch is to be believed, this was especially true of the Spartans:

> In time of war, too, they relaxed the severity of the young men's discipline, and permitted them to beautify their hair and ornament their arms and clothing, rejoicing to see them, like horses, prance and neigh for the contest. Therefore they wore their hair long as

soon as they ceased to be youths, and particularly in times of danger they took pains to have it glossy and well-combed, remembering a certain saying of Lycurgus, that a fine head of hair made the handsome more comely still, and the ugly more terrible...And when at last they were drawn up in battle array and the enemy was at hand, the king sacrificed the customary she-goat, commanded all the warriors to set garlands upon their heads.[41]

While Cunaxa didn't explicitly involve Spartans alone, they made up a significant component of the Greek contingent, with one of the chief commanders, Clearchus, himself a Spartan; moreover, Xenophon himself was a known proponent of Sparta. He even alludes to Persia's support of Sparta in his *Hellenica*, for instance.[42] Soldiers from other Greek *poleis* were likely to do their own thing to emphasize their appearance in the run up to battle. But let's get back to Cunaxa.

In the passage quoted above on the arrival of the Persians, the enemy Persians appeared on the horizon as a dust cloud, first as a giant white cloud, but then becoming something more recognizable. That mysterious cloud was followed by flashes of bronze. While Greek and Roman historians liked to highlight this sort of visual imagery, and it can sometimes be maligned as idle descriptive glossing, the dry, desert climate of Cunaxa, where average daytime high temperatures in August and September can reach 30 to 34 degrees Celsius, on a dry, dusty day, it wouldn't take much for thousands of Persian soldiers on the move to draw up tonnes of sand and debris.[43]

Sight plays a bigger role when Xenophon shifts to the combat itself, with both what Cyrus could see, and what the Greek hoplites and peltasts couldn't see, having an impact. Starting with the latter, after the Greeks had lined up and charged the Persians opposite them, they soon found themselves with the upper hand, for their foes turned and fled at the sight of the Greeks. In doing so, they abandoned their chariots which came hurtling towards the Greeks – and the Persians as it happens – at speed.[44] Then, in one swift motion, the Greeks managed to split their lines so allowing the chariots to pass through and leaving the men, for the most part, unharmed. Although Xenophon doesn't provide any details here about the depth and tightness of the Greek phalanx, that they were able to make a gap in time, so preventing significant potential injury, suggests to me that there was ample space for the men to manoeuvre and that they were a cohesive bunch. A good deal of the action would have involved men who couldn't see much beyond the men around them, however. Their movement and cohesion in this moment would have involved a good deal of trust. Perhaps they couldn't see the danger hurtling towards them, and so when the call came to move quickly and in an orderly manner in a particular direction, they would have had to trust that this was moving them away from danger and not towards it. On the other hand, those deployed at the front would have had a firsthand view of what was unfolding, and so could see what the potential dangers could be. Those at the front, whom Homer calls the *promachoi* (fighters at the front), would regularly have to face the danger and overcome it, as they would here. In fact, on this subject, writers like Xenophon and others state that some of the more experienced soldiers would be deployed at the front, and those with the most experience at the back – those who knew what was likely to come, but wouldn't turn and flee at the first hint of danger.

To get back to all these men deployed in the phalanx then, whatever fear they might have had, they trusted in their comrades, moved out of the way, and as I said just about all of them escaped unscathed. Xenophon tells us that there might have been one exception, however, a soldier who was so panic-struck by the chariots that he got himself run over. Whether that was because he could hear the chariots but not see them or because he could see it all unfold, we cannot say. That said, it's easy to imagine either possibility being the cause of his fear. Plus, Xenophon even says that a report of the battle, or episode within the battle, indicated that he didn't get hurt. Instead, the only guy who did was on the left wing and he was struck with an arrow.[45]

In contrast to the hoplites in the thick of the action, there could be the high-ranking commander located at the back. In this case, involving a large, diverse army like Cyrus', the general was likely to be stationed where he could see the action and make the decisions needed as the situation arose. Cyrus was in a position to see the action in the course of combat, and kept a careful eye, at least at the outset, on what his foes were up to. Xenophon then tells us that it was standard practice for Persian kings to be positioned in the centre at the back of the army, what they felt was the safest spot in the army, equidistant from both sides if the general needed reinforcements, and it meant that messages from any part of the army could arrive more quickly.[46] All this said, in Xenophon's telling the king moved out of this central position to his right wing, opposite Cyrus' left, which at this point in the battle was empty. The Greek hoplites who had pushed back their Persian foes had gone after them in pursuit, so leaving a noticeable gap. Owing to his position, he had a clear view. The battlefield itself, located somewhere in the environs of Baghdad, was comparatively flat, even though we don't know where it was exactly (a couple of possibilities have stood out, villages near Baghdad). The sightlines from his position, wherever it was, would have been pretty good from the back of a horse, and so he likely could have seen clearly every way, though this could have been obstructed, to some degree or other, by the other groups around him. It seems likely, however, that the same would have been true of Artaxerxes, who was situated in the centre of his army.

On the same side as the Greeks, after Cyrus saw the success of the Greek forces, he stood where he was with 600 cavalry ('table-companions', his bodyguards) to see how the battle would develop, before he decided to attack the 6,000 cavalry soldiers positioned around Artaxerxes. When he saw an opportunity, he seized it and, though it at first seemed to go well, things soon soured and his men lost their cohesion. The consequences were disastrous and he ended up losing his life, though not before he saw the king, Artaxerxes, yell out 'I see him!', and charged after him, wounding the king in the process. It was in the melee, when the two groups were embroiled, that Cyrus was struck and later died.

The Feel of Cunaxa

In this large battle involving many tens of thousands of soldiers, there was bound to be some crowding, especially as the fortunes of divergent sides and divisions within their armies waxed and waned. As I noted earlier in this chapter, the ten thousand Greeks comprised a variety of different troops types, from heavily armoured infantry and light Greek troops to heavily armoured hoplites from a variety of locales, and Xenophon's account focused largely on them. In fact, in his telling, they hardly suffered in battle, with just one man run over by a scythed chariot. Their issues were still to come on the long march home. But Xenophon seems to have overstated the case, and though their combat performance was reputable, it likely wasn't on the level that the author implies.[47] In fact, even in antiquity some disputed the performance of the Greeks, an issue which remains to this day.[48] Plutarch, for instance, blamed the Greeks for Cyrus' failure.[49]

The Greeks were deployed on the right side of Cyrus the Younger's position in the centre of the line. Opposite them were the Persian scythed chariots, as we noted earlier. The sounds emanating from the Greek side (shouts and possibly the crashing of spears on shields), especially as they charged the Persians, managed to frighten their foes so much that chariot drivers abandoned their vehicles after they were set in motion. The Greeks maintained their formation and split to allow them to move through their ranks. Once the chariots had passed, the Greeks regrouped to meet those Persians still deployed opposite them. The Persians, who had fled their chariots, couldn't bear to face the Greek charge and so caved. The Greeks set off in pursuit and killed perhaps as many as 15,000 soldiers on the Persian side.[50] One of the things the charging Greeks might have felt in these stages of combat was the thundering of the earth as they hurtled after the Persians. But the same might well have been true of the Persian chariots – the Greeks could see and hear them coming just as much as they could feel them coming. The one man who would have felt more of the chariots was the unfortunate Greek man who was run over.

Although Xenophon doesn't use the word for phalanx much in the *Anabasis*, let alone in the battle, it is a term he made particular use of, as I noted above. Indeed, for Echeverría, Xenophon gives the phalanx 'its name, and he accurately describes its nature and characteristics'.[51] In the *Hellenica* in particular, his follow-up to Thucydides' *History*, Xenophon regularly uses the term in a variety of contexts, which tells us a great deal about the potential tactile experience of combat. There are several words he uses to describe a phalanx including the Greek words for deep, dense, or solid. These words are all very visual, though the images convey a great deal about the potential closeness between soldiers within the formation. Not only did phalanxes have a particular character: they also had some particular tendencies. According to Thucydides:

> All armies are alike in this: on going into action they get forced out rather on their right wing, and one and the other overlap with this their adversary's left; because fear makes each man do his best to shelter his unarmed side with the shield of the man next him on the right, thinking that the closer the shields are locked together the better will he be protected. The man primarily responsible for this is the first upon the right wing, who is always striving to withdraw from the enemy his unarmed side; and the same apprehension makes the rest follow him.[52]

Thucydides' comments came in the midst of his discussion of the battle at Mantineia during the Peloponnesian war and it could well be a deliberate move in these very particular circumstances.[53] Yet, though this is a specific battle, he meant it to apply to larger armies in general; moreover, the Greeks at Cunaxa could be called a larger army, at least by Greek standards. That said, we don't know if this is how the hoplites at Cunaxa behaved, and Xenophon doesn't say. But Thucydides and Xenophon were contemporaries, even if Thucydides would have been much older. Plus, we know Xenophon knew Thucydides, or at least his work, well. So, if that kind of thing, the veering to the right, was a thing when Thucydides was writing, there's every reason to suppose it was a thing in Xenophon's day too, and in 401 BCE especially. In this passage, although Thucydides doesn't explicitly say that one man would be brushing up against another, in this scenario it seems a real possibility. This desire to get closer to a comrade for protection, to practically touch him, was real. And even if one man didn't touch another man, it's likely they would at least brush against their fellow soldier's shield.

The phalanx can also, in Xenophon's telling, be made, led, and the formation itself can be turned. It can also spread itself, break through, turn around, and flee.[54] His phalanxes also have left and right flanks, and a centre. The phalanxes are also firmly associated with the hoplites, and though this is often made out to be something that emerged in Archaic Greece, they are better associated with the Classical era.[55] As noted, distinctive features of their panoply included the shield, which was bigger than earlier ones (and held by one hand holding two handles), a spear, a sword, the distinctive Corinthian helmet, the breastplate and the greaves.[56] And this is to say nothing of any clothing underneath. The armour, like the shield, could be heavy, and so could have limited the agility of the hoplite, though it's not as heavy as some had earlier supposed.[57] In Krentz's reckoning, a hoplite from about 506 BCE, so a century earlier than Cunaxa, could be expected to be wearing armour and holding equipment that could weigh between 30 and 50 pounds (14 and 22 kilograms).[58]

The shield was arguably the most distinctive feature of a hoplite, and for the most part they were made with perishable materials, which is why they haven't survived in great numbers.[59] Although, as I noted, certainly one of the heavier pieces of the panoply, the Greeks do seem to have opted for lighter softwood in the construction, going for poplar and willow. Other widely available types of wood, like oak and ash, were heavy and less flexible.[60] Still, the shields were heavy enough that in Sparta standing with the shield could be used as a punishment.[61] Plus, as fit as a Greek hoplite might be, they likely couldn't hold a shield for too long, nor are they likely to have used it for much more than defence. In fact, outside of battle, the Greeks would have relied on servants to take care of their equipment and baggage carts to transport them. So, a big part of the tactile part of this and any battle was coming to grips with holding the shield.

Marching on One's Stomach

To this point, I haven't said much about the impact of taste and smell on this battle. While it undoubtedly would have had a marked impact, from the perspective of these soldiers, the long march back to Greece through the Persian Empire was more pronounced in this regard. The march posed some significant challenges to the soldiers, particularly with respect to getting food and water. While I don't want to say too much about it here, I want to highlight a few of the challenges, which have been described so well by Lee.[62]

Some of this food would have been cooked, so the soldiers would have been lugging around some cooking materials, with perhaps individual soldiers carrying personal items, while larger things, like cauldrons and pans, were carried as part of the baggage train.[63] Of course, if food was to be cooked, they'd need fuel to feed the fires, so soldiers would also need tools to get the wood and use it – and proximity to firewood would also be important. They'd also need tools to start the fires in the first place.

Usually, Greek soldiers would take two meals, a morning one and an evening one, though mealtimes weren't always regular.[64] Breakfasts might have been first thing in the morning, but they weren't always. At the same time, the dinner could be in the afternoon. It could also be in early evening. There was some structure to these morning or evening meals, if the conditions allowed. It also offered an opportunity to promote unity and cohesion amongst the men – and for the lower ranking to mix amongst the commanders, and bring up important details if need be in relative ease. For example,

> While Xenophon was eating, two young men ran up to him. Everyone knew that, if they had a military matter to discuss, they could approach him during mealtimes.[65]

The staples of the men's diet would have been grain, whether barley or wheat. With their grain, the soldiers might eat things like cheese, olives, garlic, and onions, much of which was easier to transport.[66] Meat too would have played a role, depending on circumstances. As for drinking, water and wine were obviously important. The wine was usually watered down, while the water wasn't always safe. Plus, the men are likely to have preferred drinking wine anyway, which they could buy or take from any locals they came across.

All this transporting of food and supplies, and its preparation, might seem straightforward enough, but the march lasted for many months, and the terrain they traversed varied widely. According to Xenophon, 10,400 men had set out for Cunaxa in 401 BCE, and by 399 BCE only 6,000 had made it back. Some items would have been easier to get in certain locations than others. In some cases, the need for food and drink pushed them further. When they got to the mountains and there was considerable snow, as was the case in Armenia, eating and drinking could be a significant challenge, as Xenophon himself tells us. To give a few examples from their entry into Corduene, which is described in Book 4 of Xenophon's *Anabasis*, when the Greeks fall upon the Carduchians, they fled with their families into the mountains. The Greeks then entered their homes in their villages and took the supplies they needed.[67] A bit later, the Greeks had a chance to rest and enjoy the Carduchian food and wine, which was plentiful, at least for a time.[68] While marching in Armenia, they came across some more villages full of supplies, cattle, grain, wine, raisins, and vegetables.[69] Before they knew it, however, winter fell and the soldiers found themselves marching through mountainous terrain while trying to manoeuvre through deep snow. At this point in the proceedings, the winter soon took its toll, especially when it came to eating and drinking:

> The whole of the following day was spent marching through snow, and a lot of the men suffered from hunger faintness. Xenophon, who was bringing up the rear, kept coming across men who had fallen by the wayside and did not know what was wrong with them, until someone who had met it before told him that the men were obviously suffering from hunger faintness and would be able to get to their feet if they had something to eat. So Xenophon searched through the baggage train and handed out anything edible he found or sent those who were capable of running to give the food to those who were ill – and after they had eaten something they got to their feet and carried on.[70]

In the end, only a small sample, but a good indication of the trouble with taste and smell, or as I've construed them here, eating and drinking.[71]

Though most of this chapter has concentrated on the sights, sounds, and feel of Greek soldiers in combat, especially involving phalanxes and in particular here at Cunaxa, these other senses are important too. To survive a battle, getting enough to eat was integral. The same was true for fluids after combat, when sweaty soldiers would need to rehydrate. In short, pitched battle in Classical Greece was a full sensory experience.

Chapter 2

The Battle of Issus (333 BCE)

From the fifth century BCE into the fourth, war gradually became a technical skill in the Greek world.[1] There were lots of changes in the fourth century especially, and this included the rise of career officers, the increased use of mercenaries, and the establishment of elite units often trained by professional drillmasters.[2] The general too had become the most important part of an army, and the changing nature of Greek warfare demanded generals with cerebral skills.[3] The physical presence of the commander was less important than his ability to manage the course of battle. Eventually the Hellenistic thinkers suggested that the general's rash personal daring could hurt the cause.

The individual and army who for many ushered in the Hellenistic world did not lead armies this way. Alexander the Great's practice fell somewhere in the middle between the general as battle manager and the general as warrior leading from the front. He and one of his famous victories, the Battle of Issus, are the subject of this chapter,.

There are any number of ways we could explore the sensory experiences of this battle, but I will focus especially on the visual, in something of a break from the rest of the chapters in this book. Issus was a battle for the eyes, for what one could, and couldn't, see had a significant role in the battle's outcome. After providing a brief overview, I'll look at the topography of the battlefield and Macedonian attempts to limit the vision of their Greek mercenary opponents fighting in the Persian army. Then I'll turn to Alexander's own positioning over the course of the battle, from what impact his place on the right had on his attempts at observing his men, to how the location in close proximity to a mountain range limited the usual means of communication in battle, namely the use of sound (see Image 10).[4] Along those lines, I will discuss how what Alexander might have seen in this battle influenced how he managed its outcome.[5] Finally, I will look at Alexander's very deliberate and visual charge at the king Darius, who in turn made a clear retreat in view of his own army.

Background

The Battle of Issus, waged between Alexander's Macedonian army and Darius' Persians, was fought in 333 BCE on a narrow plain between mountain and sea northeast of modern Iskenderun, Turkey (see Image 8).[6] The Persians had lost a year earlier at the River Granicus, and their king was now determined to face Alexander's army in person. Interestingly enough, although the two armies had come quite close to each other not long before they met in battle, they couldn't see one another, separated as they were by a mountain range. Darius' vast army, composed of all the forces of Persis and Media along with some Greek mercenaries, might have numbered between 100,000 and 150,000 men, while Alexander's might have numbered 40,000.[7] Our sources for this battle are significant: we have the accounts of Plutarch, Justin, Polybius, Diodorus, Curtius, and Arrian, of which Justin's and Plutarch's are shorter, while the others are more substantial.[8] There is also, of course, the beautiful mosaic from Pompeii.

Though the sources are plentiful, they are anything but straightforward, which is most apparent if we look at how some of the varied literary sources treat Alexander's tactics and deployment. One author from whom we have very little is Callisthenes, an historian who accompanied Alexander in Asia, and one whom Polybius seems to loathe. In particular, Polybius disputes Callisthenes' account of Alexander's advance (he doesn't specify where, exactly) because, in his mind, the topography of the battlefield does not fit with the alleged number of troops at Alexander's disposal. For example, Polybius asserts that 'it would, therefore, have been considerably better to form a proper double or quadruple phalanx, for which it was not impossible to find marching room and which it would have been quite easy to get into order of battle expeditiously enough, as his scouts informed him in good time, warning him of the approach of the enemy'.[9] Polybius' biggest issue with Callisthenes is his record of the length of Alexander's line. Indeed, Polybius is most rancorous when

Callisthenes is describing the formation of Darius' or Alexander's armies, and their employment. This explains why Polybius criticizes the alleged emplacement of the troops in front of the phalanx with the river so close and the troop numbers so high. He adds the following statement: 'For to be really useful cavalry should be at the most eight deep, and between each unit there must be a space equal in length to the front of a unit so that there may be no difficulty in wheeling and facing around'.[10]

Justin, who may have been writing in the third century (CE), provides only a summary account of the battle.[11] His account, written in Latin, shows no concern with those issues that are so important to Polybius. Quintus Curtius, who was writing in the second half of the first century (CE) and again also in Latin, is more concerned with the character and actions of Alexander, and in this battle Darius as well, than with technical military minutiae.[12] So, we find a brief description of the topography of Alexander's camp followed by Alexander's concerns over the start of the battle.[13] With the characters of Alexander and Darius central to the narrative, it is not surprising that for Curtius emotions play such a prominent role in his description of the battle.[14] Diodorus, who was writing in Greek in the first century BCE, describes the Battle of Issus.[15] Diodorus, like Curtius, is also unconcerned with the technical concerns of warfare though he too has written a vivid account of the battle. Diodorus is concerned with issues such as the bravery of certain soldiers and, like Curtius, the emotional impact of the battle on its participants. So, we find descriptions such as this, which are evocative but rather general:

> By now the rest of the cavalry on both sides was engaged and many were killed as the battle raged indecisively because of the evenly matched fighting qualities of the two sides. The scales inclined now one way, now another, as the lines swayed alternately forward and backward. No javelin cast or sword thrust lacked its effect as the crowded ranks offered a ready target. Many fell with wounds received as they faced the enemy and their fury held to the last breath, so that life failed them sooner than courage.[16]

That passage is indicative of the stirring nature of Diodorus' battle-narrative; the diction, the metaphor, and the imagery, among other qualities, all make for an intoxicating description. But, for all its charm, it too is short of technical military detail. Plutarch, who wrote in the late first century and early second century CE in Greek, also described the battle, at least in some detail, in his biography of Alexander.[17] Given the genre, it is perhaps understandable that the focus of his description is Alexander's actions; Darius too garners a fair bit of attention. But the same issues that arise in the narratives of Justin, Curtius, and Diodorus also arise with Plutarch. Although both Curtius' and Diodorus' narratives are vivid and detailed – Justin's at least relates the principal characters and the outcome, and Plutarch's includes some interesting material about Alexander's and Darius' motives during the battle – all four are short of technical military material and as such would probably have drawn Polybius' scorn. Arrian is probably the exception.

Although usually the high watermark of ancient Alexander narratives, Arrian, like the others, wasn't a contemporary and instead was writing in the middle of the second century CE. He was, in fact, an accomplished general, who also wrote a short tract on tactics, and another brief work on how to defeat the Alans, a steppe people who caused the Romans trouble in the Caucasus and beyond in the second century CE. Like Polybius, he wrote in Greek. He also consciously modelled his work on Xenophon. Though dating to the Roman imperial era, however, Arrian had access to sources we no longer have, and for this reason and some of those given above, he's usually considered the best of the lot.

Arrian describes the Battle of Issus in considerable detail. In the beginning of his narrative Arrian points out that Darius picked a location for battle that was suitable for his troops. Shortly thereafter Arrian notes that it did not work quite as Darius had hoped: 'some divine power led Darius into the very position where his cavalry did not much help him, nor the number of his men and javelins and arrows, where he could make no display even of the splendour of his army, but delivered the victory easily to Alexander and his force'.[18] Although Arrian is attempting to alert his audience to the fact that things were going to turn out in Alexander's favour, he also notes incidentally that the terrain did not suit some of Darius' troops; Arrian, perhaps subconsciously, has made a connection between terrain and troop disposition. This same issue arises not long after for he notes that the terrain into which Darius' forces were headed would put their numerically superior army at a significant disadvantage.[19] In fact, the description of the battle order of the respective forces takes up a huge portion of Arrian's narrative and his interest in military matters, and in particular battle-orders and formations, is apparent as the following passage suggests:

> The foreign mercenaries were drawn up in support of the whole line. But as his phalanx did not seem very solid on his right, and the Persians seemed likely to overlap them considerably there, he ordered his two squadrons of the Companions from the centre, that from Anthemus, commanded by Peroedes...and that called the Leugaean, under Pantordanus...to transfer unobserved to the right wing. He brought over the archers and some of the Agrianians and Greek mercenaries to the front of his right and so extended his phalanx to out-flank the Persian wing. For since the troops posted on the heights had not descended, but on a sally made by the Agrianians and a few archers at Alexander's order, had been easily dislodged from the foothills and had fled to the summit.[20]

This extended quotation is only part of a longer discussion of Alexander's attempts to counter the actions of Darius in respect to the topography of the battlefield. The rest of the battle narrative is in fact filled with discussion of the actions of the various components of the two battlelines. Thus, despite Arrian's claims that the outcome of the battle had been pre-ordained by some divine power, the narrative of the battle itself suggests that the outcome hinged on the generalship of Alexander, his superior tactics, and especially the phalanx. This interpretation of Arrian's intentions in his narrative is encapsulated at 2.10.6:

> There the action was severe, the Greeks tried to push off the Macedonians into the river and to restore victory to their own side who were already in flight, while the Macedonians sought to

rival the success of Alexander, which was already apparent, and to preserve the reputation of the phalanx, whose sheer invincibility had hitherto been on everyone's lips.[21]

Unfortunately, despite the battle's fame, the contradictory details found in the different accounts make reconstruction difficult.[22] One of the main points that the different accounts differ on is Alexander and his army's deployment. Although the great number of sources can be a blessing, it can also be a curse, for they disagree wildly on the numbers available on both sides. What they do agree on, however, is that the Persians vastly outnumbered the Macedonians. It also seems that the two sides met rather hastily, with the Persians, as in past encounters both more recent and more ancient, confident in their numbers.[23]

The Macedonian Army

Before we go further with Arrian and Issus, a little more background on the Macedonian military is in order. Arrian's comments above highlight the reputation of Alexander's, though really Philip's, Macedonian army. Macedonian armies had phalanxes, like Xenophon's from the previous chapter, but they weren't the same. There were a number of important developments that took place in the fourth century BCE, including an increase in the use of professionals along with an increase in the size of, well, most things – bigger siege towers and bigger phalanxes, for instance.[24] Other kinds of soldiers – not heavily-armed hoplites – took a greater role in combat, like light infantry and cavalry, with the latter particularly important in Macedon. Technology changed too. Siege machines and artillery were the subject of significant developments, with Philip II sometimes credited with creating the torsion catapult, and Alexander later with a stone thrower. A big part of this was the role of military engineers. The scale of these developments were such that they have been characterized as a military revolution.[25]

A big driver of the changes in Macedon was Philip II, whose efforts have also been called revolutionary.[26] In his case, a big inspiration might have been the fourth century BCE Athenian general Iphicrates.[27] Some of the issues he faced was how to equip a mass of infantry.

Pressing conditions seem to have impelled his response, with the infantry panoply being lighter at first as a result of financial troubles. As this improved, more money was spent on equipment which in turn grew bigger.[28]

Regarding more specific changes, Philip II brought infantry into a dense formation and gave them 15 to 18-foot-long pike-like sarissas. This Macedonian formation was denser than its Classical Greek forebearer, especially when the soldiers locked their shields.[29] He most likely changed how they fought and improved their training.[30] Philip also made his soldiers professionals; they were given regular pay, which meant that troops could operate year-round.[31] Ultimately, the Macedonian army could be considered a standing army. As a result of all this, the Macedonian phalanx was good enough to hold an enemy phalanx in position until their much-vaunted cavalry finished them off. Through a variety of things, combined arms included, Macedonian phalanxes were incredibly successful.[32]

The army that Alexander inherited was the much reformed one his father had whipped into shape.[33] It was a competitive entity too, with performance determining where you got to be in the battle line. In general, the king would be positioned on the extreme right of the cavalry along with the best troops.[34] But he also went to considerable lengths to encourage the competitive spirit of the soldiers. Lendon described 'Alexander's ceaseless effort to reinforce the spirit of competition in his army' thus:

> The king offered prizes for unusual feats of bravery, he watched for the brave deeds of his men in battle, and after victory he visited the wounded to hear them recount their exploits...All Greeks were competitive, but rivalry among the Macedonians had a rawer edge.[35]

Alexander's Macedonian army was varied, with soldiers hailing from a variety of places, including, along with the Macedonians themselves, Agrianian mountaineers (from northwest Bulgaria), archers (some Macedonian, some Thracian, others Cretan), and then cavalry from Thrace, the Peloponnesus, and central Greece.[36] Collectively, the

Macedonian component was a modest proportion of the overall army, with a significant change coming in 330 BCE, when soldiers from Greece and Macedon played an increasingly smaller role.[37] That said, Alexander never seems to have sought a wholesale replacement of the Macedonian component of the military.

The standard shape of Alexander's line gave each of the three overarching parts, the left, centre, and right, specific roles: the left had a defensive role, the centre was tasked with maintaining the position, and the right, where Alexander would be positioned, was responsible for attacking.[38] Heckel notes:

> he enticed the enemy into attempting a flanking move on its left wing, thereby separating the wing from the centre left. This point he then attacked with his own right wing. The right hand of the phalanx fixed the enemy just beyond the centre, while the Companions exploited the developing gap on the enemy left and wheeled to take the broken formation in the flank. The hypaspists acted as the hinge, keeping contact with both phalanx and the cavalry and, once the flank attack began to throw the enemy into confusion, intermingling with the horsemen as the fighting turned to slaughter. But for the difficulties of the terrain at Issus, all three of Alexander's major battles against the Persians followed this general pattern.[39]

It's worth returning to the competitiveness that Alexander's formations encouraged, a point which Lendon stresses. Different units within the Macedonian army regularly competed to outdo each other in a variety of capacities with the aim of promotion, or even preventing the possibility of demotion.[40] Quintus Curtius lays it out well in a context outside of the battlefield when Alexander was in the process of rebuilding Tanais as another Alexandria.

> The work was completed with such speed, that seventeen days after the fortifications were raised the buildings of the city were also finished. There had been great rivalry of the soldiers with one another, that each band – for the work had been divided – might be the first to show the completion of its task.[41]

It's also worth highlighting this competitiveness, stressed by Lendon, before turning to the Battle of Issus itself. For Lendon, this competitiveness is tied to the pull of Homer, the most important author for war writing in the ancient world. Many also see Homer's world as a competitive one, with the glory of a warrior tied to his performance in battle in front of his peers.[42] The better a warrior performed in combat, the better the prizes he would get for his success. The *Iliad* itself is very much tied to this – the poem is filled with fighting, which, for many, provides a composite view comprising warfare of Homer's own day (eighth century BCE) and the late Bronze Age – the end of the Trojan War is dated to 1184 BCE – his poem depicts.[43] The poem is centred on the glory of a hero, and in particular Achilles. That said, all of the warrior heroes that fill its pages follow a heroic code, which is built on performance in single combat, where they fight to enhance their reputation and demonstrate their skill.

The heroic code of Homeric warriors was tied to their honour or respect, their *time*. During combat (though it could be elsewhere too), they hope to display excellence, *arete*, during a moment of excellence, *aristeia*. If they do well enough in these contexts, they'll get a prize, *geras*, as the Greek heroes at the start of the *Iliad* did. Though Lendon might overstate the impact of Homer on later eras, the poet and his poem did leave its mark on Alexander. When Alexander and his army marched across the Hellespont into Persian territory and he set out on his great war of conquest, one of his first stops was at Troy, or so Plutarch would have us believe. Plutarch says:

> Then, going up to Ilium, he sacrificed to Athena and poured libations to the heroes. Furthermore, the gravestone of Achilles he anointed with oil, ran a race by it with his companions, naked, as is the custom, and then crowned it with garlands, pronouncing the hero happy in having, while he lived, a faithful friend, and after death, a great herald of his fame. As he was going about and viewing the sights of the city, someone asked him if he wished to see the lyre of Paris. 'For that lyre,' said Alexander, 'I care very little; but I would gladly see that of Achilles, to which he used to sing the glorious deeds of brave men.'[44]

If Plutarch is right, the poem and its most famous character, Achilles, played a big role in Alexander's consciousness. Why that matters here is that it helps us to understand the important role that sight plays in his approach to combat. Over the course of Greek antiquity ancient views on what it meant to be a general changed considerably.[45] The Homeric leader led from the front, sought glory, and often opted for single combat. In the Classical era, generalship itself emerges due to the increasing complexity of the battlefield, and the need arose for a leader to organize the army rather than fight himself from the front. Some generals still did, but aside from Sparta, the generals were still amateurs.

While that might seem representative of many if not most combatants, in the transitionary period from the Classical Greek world to the Hellenistic one, a great deal was changing regarding how armies fought, and even what they looked like. This included a probable shift in how contemporaries thought generals should perform in combat. Where earlier leaders, Homeric ones especially, though Archaic and Classical ones too, were usually believed to take firsthand roles not only in directing men and units, but also in the hand-to-hand combat itself, as armies got bigger, increasingly the role of the general was as a battle manager, positioned at the back of the battle lines telling his men where to go.[46] By the fourth century, the generals played a leading role in Greek warfare, and they were usually absent from the front of the line. With the rise of the Macedonians and the increased size of Hellenistic armies, the role of the generals changed even more: the general became more professional, and his role as manager increased, and his safety on the battlefield came to supersede any desire for feats of personal daring. It is this world in which we find Alexander, where the battlefield manager was increasing in importance.

The Phalanx at Issus

Let's get back to Issus. After some pre-battle rituals, the two sides drew up for battle. For the Persians, their cavalry was situated on the right wing by the sea, Darius was situated in the centre, two groups of Greek mercenary hoplites were drawn on either side, and some cavalry and light infantry were on the left in the foothills (see Image 9).[47] As for the Macedonians, the allied and mercenary cavalry were on Alexander's left, Alexander led the Companion cavalry on the right, and next to them the hypaspists and the sarissa phalanx, and on their left the mercenary Greek infantry.[48] The two most important positions for us, however, are those of Darius and Alexander, to which we will return in a bit.

When the two armies had drawn up for battle, Alexander's Macedonians were disadvantaged not only because of their numerical inferiority, but also because they seem to have drawn up just across one of the two rivers that ran through the field of battle. An integral part of the success of any phalanx, Classical or Hellenistic, was the integrity of the line, and changes in topography could undermine this. At Issus, just like the earlier battle at the River Granicus,[49] there seems to have been a noticeable difference in elevation between the north side where the Persian forces were deployed, and the south side where the Macedonians were.[50] Crossing the river meant some disruption to the Macedonian infantry, especially its phalanx, though the scale of the difficulty has engendered debate among scholars, with some arguing that Ptolemy and Callisthenes exaggerated the crossing.[51] Although the river might not have been mighty, the banks were precipitous enough that the Macedonians would have trouble maintaining the integrity of their phalanx as they advanced from a lower position to a higher one. The perceived difficulty in this crossing has led some to argue that the Macedonians didn't even use sarissas in this battle as they would have been unmanageable.[52] And fair enough. These sarissas were inordinately long, at 15 to 18 feet each as noted above.[53] And yet, some of the sources, though not Polybius, imply that Alexander's phalanx struggled a little as it tried to cross the river. This might entirely be down to the precipitous banks of the river. But if the crossing is difficult enough to warrant comment by some sources, to my mind this implies that they had sarissas in hand as they crossed, which would have made things even more difficult.[54] The men's bottom halves would have been wet and soggy from the water, which they could feel. Plus, with all these men crossing the river, water would inevitably get splashed and hands and weapons would get wet, so making them hard to hold.

While trying to hold a massive spear would likely complicate the phalanx's movement in this uneven topography, the long sarissas could still be of some value. In ordinary circumstances, the men in the front rank would have held their sarissas at waist level.[55] On occasion, however, soldiers might hold their spears up and in the direction of their foes' upper bodies.[56] In a case like this, where the position of one side was higher than another's, it would offer some of the cover they would need to cross safely, and this seems to have been what the Macedonian phalangites did at Issus.[57] According to Curtius, 'there was great bloodshed; for the two armies were so close together that shield struck against shield, and they directed their tips at each other's faces'.[58] It's hard to imagine how to get face-to-face (or shield-to-shield) with 18-foot sarissas, and Curtius doesn't explain it. This comment could well be due to his lack of familiarity with these kinds of soldiers in action – he was probably writing in the first century CE. As noted, this wasn't the ordinary practice. There's plenty of direct and indirect evidence that the majority of wounds sustained in combat against sarissas were to various parts of the body besides the head and neck. Blows to the face from a sarissa would usually be fatal, and the relative abundance of those who walked away from such an encounter is suggestive.[59] And so, when faced with a foe in an elevated position who was familiar with Macedonian sarissas, going against convention and aiming at the face would have made sense, especially amongst a group of phalangites with a competitive spirit eager to match the success of Alexander's cavalry to their right.[60]

Sarissas were an awesome sight on their own. If you stood opposite them and one was coming towards your face, let alone one hit the mark, you wouldn't be able to see much else. It was Plutarch who probably said it best, when referring to Lucius Aemillius at Pydna (fought between Rome and Macedon in 168 BCE):

As the attack began, Aemilius came up and found that the Macedonian battalions had already planted the tips of their long spears in the shields of the Romans, who were thus prevented from reaching them with their swords. And when he saw that the rest of the Macedonian troops also were drawing their targets from their shoulders round in front of them, and with long spears sat at one level were withstanding his shield-bearing troops, and saw too the strength of their interlocked shields and the fierceness of their onset, amazement and fear took possession of him, and he felt that he had never seen a sight more fearful; often in after times he used to speak of his emotions at that time and of what he saw. [61]

In this part of the battle, then, when the two sides were locked together and progress was slow, restricting the sight of your opponents could make a real difference.

Alexander on the Right

From the Macedonian infantry in the centre, let's shift to Alexander and the Companion cavalry on the right. Battles are complex affairs, and their memorialists have struggled for centuries to make sense of the chaos, the toing-and-froing, and the varied experiences.[62] Indeed, for some, in pre-modern battles like these Hellenistic era ones, once battle had started, there was little a commander could hope to do to change its course.

At Issus, as we noted above, the number of combatants from both sides was incredible, and the difficulty in managing such a large number of soldiers would have been apparent. If battle truly is non-linear, then in a battle like this one at Issus it would have been particularly difficult for a general to bring order to the chaos, especially if they led from the front – that is from a position that gave them a very narrow view of the action. And Alexander was famed for this leading-from-the-front heroic leadership.[63] Though we don't know the precise location of the battle, it does seem to have been fought on a fairly small plain between the sea and the mountains to the northeast of modern Iskenderun between two small rivers. While the land levelled out closer to the sea, as noted with respect to crossing of the river, some positions were elevated. This would have made getting a full view of the battle impossible from several locations. If Alexander had been placed at the back of his army in the centre, he would have had a very restricted view in nearly every direction, save to the east and the Amanus Mountains.

The same is true, at least to some degree, of Darius' position in the centre and in the rear of the Persian army: though there was a little more visibility, in spots, around the field of battle from there, and his position standing in the chariot allowed him to see over many of his men, his view was restricted. As he had been previously, and would be again at Gaugamela, Alexander was deployed on the right of his battle line.[64] In this case that meant in the foothills, from which he would have had no visibility to his rear, but a nearly unobstructed view towards the entirety of the Persian army and the bulk of his own – a vastly superior view to Darius'. Alexander might well have had good tactical reasons for positioning himself on the right of his battle line, but in this particular circumstance it also served important ends from the perspective of battle management: he could see what was happening if he was deployed in that position, something he couldn't do if he adopted Darius' position to the rear, or went to the far left against the sea (see Image 10).

Of course, it's all well and good to be able to see what's going on in battle and to adjust the formations and movements as necessary, it's quite another thing to be able to carry this off in the thick of battle. If there's one thing the debate over the historicity of the pre-battle speeches in classical historians taught me, it's the difficulty in hearing a speech with a big crowd under most conditions. These challenges apply to the thick of battle too, when it would have been extremely difficult for Alexander to communicate audibly to his comrades. Once the groans of anguished and angry soldiers, the assorted war cries, and the clashing of weapons were thrown into the mix, however, it would have been darn nigh impossible to hear commands clearly.[65] The particular location of this battle posed another problem, for the mountains surrounding the field amplified the sound so making for a distracting echo. Though this doesn't seem to have stopped the Macedonians from using instruments like trumpets to convey some instructions, at least at the start, in the chaos of this battle, sight could play a much bigger role than sound.[66] Indeed, although invariably guilty of some rhetorical embellishment, Curtius' words convey well this difficulty:

the Macedonians [made] a sound too loud for their numbers, since they were echoed by the mountain heights and huge forests; for surrounding rocks and trees always send back with increased din whatever sound they have received. Alexander went on ahead of his foremost standards, repeatedly checking his men by a gesture of his hand.[67]

Although Curtius was mistaken about the trees, what he said about the rocks was undoubtedly true. Macedonians, like other people in the ancient Mediterranean world, had a distinctive battle expression. They would often clash their sarissa against their shield to generate a particular kind of noise. Despite the loudness, the sources imply that Alexander was able to watch the course of the battle as it unfolded and deploy different components as necessary.[68] And in Curtius' words, Alexander managed this in part – and presumably before his charge – using hand gestures, which at least for those commanders in close proximity might well have worked.

The Charge

One of the most distinctive pieces of evidence for this battle is the famed Alexander mosaic from Pompeii (see Image 11). In that scene, we find the climax of one of the most remarkable parts of the battle, Alexander's charge at Darius and the latter's subsequent retreat. Alexander's charge is the next significant visual stage of this battle, and it illustrates well the general's place in evolving views of Greek military leadership and his continued preference for heroic generalship.

Alexander led Macedon in the transitionary period between the Classical and the Hellenistic. Battle management might have been the order of the day near the end of the fourth century on, but it hadn't taken hold fully while Alexander was on his campaign of conquest. In Alexander's first three big victories, Chaeronea, Granicus, and Issus, he took the same position: on the far side of the line with the Companion cavalry. He would take it later at Gaugamela.[69]

Scholars usually draw attention to Alexander's charge at Darius himself.[70] While Alexander had been deployed in this position before, he'd never charged the enemy chief in the same way. Although the battle had in many respects started off as any other battle, in Arrian's words, though 'he continued to lead on in line, at marching pace at first...he now had Darius' force in view'.[71] When the opportunity arose, Alexander charged at Darius in full view of both armies: while it was certainly meant to lower the resolve of the Persian army, the withdrawal of Darius would only prove effective if his army could see him withdrawing. Moreover, as Curtius himself implies, Darius made a good target: his elevated position on a chariot made him an easy target for the Macedonians.[72] For Diodorus, while the battle raged, Alexander looked around desperately trying to find Darius, a point brought up by Curtius.[73] After finding and charging the king, Alexander managed to turn the king and his men into flight[74], and when the Persians saw this, they soon gave up their attack.[75] Most of the casualties came in this stage of the battle, with the Persians turning tail.[76]

Seeing is Believing

The Macedonian army represented, in some respects, the next phase in a series of changes in the Greek army, which had included the incorporation of an increasingly diverse military force, that made full use of combined arms. I hinted at this above. But one of the most distinctive and impressive components was its cavalry, which Alexander himself led. Heavy cavalry were designed to disrupt the enemy in a rapid, damaging charge. At speed, heavy cavalry charging at full speed would be an awe-inspiring sight.[77] A good way to disrupt these charges was by holding up bristling spears at the charging cavalry, for conventional wisdom has it that horses aren't keen, for obvious reasons, on charging at sharp objects.[78] At Chaeronea, a battle in which Alexander fought alongside his father in 338 BCE, most ancient accounts had it that Alexander and his cavalry charged the Theban Sacred Band, a renowned infantry group, so leading to victory. Scholars have doubted this because they doubted that horses would be prepared to charge at infantry with long spears like this.

As it happens, however, horses can be trained to overcome these sorts of conditions. As Sears and Willekes have noted, horses already do plenty of things that horses, in the wild, aren't accustomed to, like allowing riders on their backs. Plus, horses are herd animals who like to stay with the group, and they tend to follow the lead horse, the alpha male, if circumstances allow. Even better, horses have long been manipulated to take advantage of these conditions through their training, a point which Xenophon himself drew attention to.[79] In other words, if these conditions are met, they'll overcome any other misgivings they might have – like the sight of bristling weapons.[80] But there's additional evidence from that particular battle, Chaeronea, in the form of the skeletal evidence, which I touched on in Chapter 1. A few hundred bodies have been excavated from the battlefield at Chaeronea, and their remains reveal plenty of insight into how they might have (and likely did) died.[81] It seems the majority of the men, all potentially Thebans because of where they were buried, were killed by blows from above, the kind of blows likely to come from those attacking on horseback.[82]

For horses, like men, sight could be a possible obstacle to certain attacks and manoeuvres, but one that could be overcome with the necessary training. As we will see in the next chapter, which is focused on Cannae, soldiers too, regardless of their origins (Spartan, Persian, Carthaginian, Roman) are likely to have needed training to overcome any inhibitions on the field of battle, particularly when it came to the use of weapons against another human. So, to get back to sight and this battle, Issus, sight wasn't just an issue for this and other battles' human participants: it mattered to horses too. Alexander's charge required his horses overcoming certain visual obstacles: deployed against Alexander and his Companion cavalry were some heavily armed infantry, the mercenary Kardakes. As it happens, the horses weren't fazed by the sight of these hoplite-like soldiers deployed in a phalanx; instead, they quickly turned them into flight.[83] In the end, Alexander won another big victory, and Darius withdrew, much of his family now Macedonian prisoners.

Conclusion

To this point in his career, Alexander had been a visual commander. In his previous encounters, Alexander made a concerted effort to ride along the front of his line encouraging individual men, just as he did here at Issus. Not only was it important to the men so called out, but also to Alexander himself: the audience helped bolster his reputation amongst his men. The importance of the visual to Alexander didn't only come during the battle's course, but also during its aftermath; as he was wont to do, Alexander made a point of personally visiting each one of the soldiers wounded in the encounter, or so Arrian tells us.[84] It was important to be seen bolstering the spirit of the men after a hard-fought battle.[85]

Just as Alexander was a visual-orientated general, so Issus was a feast for the eyes. The location restricted movement, the Macedonian phalangites were closely packed together, and so they abandoned usual practice and directed their sarissas at the faces of their Greek opposites. Alexander, deployed on the right, had a much better view of the action from his elevated action; moreover, the echoing of the mountains meant he had to manage his army using visual cues. Finally, to make his very visual charge against Darius, Alexander and the horses that bore his cavalry had to overcome the daunting sight of the outstretched spears of the Kardakes.

Part II

The Roman World

Chapter 3

The Battle of Cannae (216 BCE)

In the middle of summer in 216 BCE, the forces of Hannibal Barca trudged along towards the small Italian town of Cannae. These soldiers, to this point wildly successful in their campaign in Italy, found themselves running low on supplies. Their intel indicated that the Romans kept a hearty store of goods in and around Cannae. So, Hannibal made a beeline for the town with a view to securing the merchandise. This successful move caused alarm amongst the Romans, who raced to intercept, with no less than two consuls, eight legions, and a proportional number of allies. Once the two armies were encamped, the Roman consuls debated facing Hannibal now or later: Paullus advocated later, Varro advocated now. To Rome's great peril, Varro won the day thanks to the system implemented in those rare scenarios where both consuls were present on the field of battle: they alternated command daily. So, while Rome seemed poised to avoid a direct clash with Hannibal, something the Punic general was keen on, the next day Varro was in charge, and he wanted to end this conflict then and there. Thus, on a hot day in August, the 2nd to be precise, the two sides drew up for battle. The Romans lined up in their traditional *triplex acies* (triple line) formation along the Aufidus river. Within a few hours, 40–50,000 Romans lay dead in one of Rome's most famous defeats.

Most of the details of the battle, its participants – Hannibal, the Roman army – and its principal sources, Polybius and Livy, have been established for a long time now, and so it's fair to wonder whether it's still possible to say anything novel about this battle, let alone any other ancient battle. There are plenty of works on Roman maniples and tactics, Hannibal's generalship, or the demographic challenges the Romans did or did not have in the wake of this war. We've even seen work on how the Second Punic War and its battles, even this one, might have been experienced by its participants. Despite this, I want to argue that there is more that we can tease out about ancient wars and battles, even Cannae, if we look at the total experience of their participants. In this chapter, I provide an overview of the sources before turning to the run up to the battle. Then, I'll describe some highlights of the battle as they relate to three of the commonly accepted senses: sight, sound, and touch. Although I'll be highlighting the senses individually, it's often the case that they blend and interact, as we'll see: for Roman war engaged all the senses. It's worth stressing too that it's not just a case of applying sensory literary flourishes to descriptions of combat, but contextualizing them.[1] At the end, I'll touch on the outstanding senses, and highlight aspects of the siege of New Carthage.

Sources

The two main sources for this battle are the Greek historian Polybius and the Roman historian Livy. Polybius was writing in the second century BCE in (unsurprisingly) Greek, while Livy was writing at the end of the first century BCE in Latin. Although they were both secular, classical, historians writing in the grand tradition of Herodotus and Thucydides, their approaches differed. Polybius had been on the Greek side against Rome during a later conflict between Macedon and its allies and Rome. He, like his side, were defeated, and Polybius became a Roman prisoner who was sent back to Rome. There, he befriended the Scipio family, including, especially, Scipio Aemilianus. This gave Polybius privileged insight into the growing Roman behemoth, which he used with aplomb in his *History*, an account of Rome's remarkable rise to power. Polybius' *History* survives only in parts, but the portion on the second Punic War is one of them. Polybius was, by his own admission, a cantankerous historian, who often lambasted outright his fellow historians who failed at their jobs, at least in his eyes, which we saw in action in Chapter 2. Because, in part, Polybius had been a general, he also put a lot of stock in tactics and battle formations, and it was because of mistakes in discussing this sort of material that he was particularly angry at fellow authors. He even wrote a work on tactics, though it no longer survives.

Livy, writing much later, wrote something else entirely, his *Ab Urbe Condita*, or 'from the Founding of the City', a history of Rome from its foundation to the present day. It starts in the murky days of early Rome, from Aeneas, the refugee from Troy who fled the Greek sack of the famed city, on to the twins, Romulus and Remus, who founded the city, and beyond. Like Polybius, his work survives only in part, the first few books in particular, then many of the middle books that deal with events in and around the Punic Wars. In fact, some of Livy's material that deals with those conflicts survives where the comparable section from Polybius is lost; moreover, Livy used Polybius as a source for some of his discussion, which we can see by comparing some parts of their works. But Livy didn't simply copy Polybius' material and paste it into his own. Rather, he took those bits he wanted to shape his narrative, sometimes bringing in additional sources. Of the extant parts of his work, the Hannibalic War, which constitutes books 20–29, is sometime held up as the most impressive part.[2] Livy's work is especially useful for us because of the attention he devotes to the emotive side of the conflict.

There are some other sources for the conflict – and the wider war. Archaeology has the most potential for furthering our understanding, and there has been all sorts of new, exciting work on the battlefields of the ancient Mediterranean world, but quite a lot remains to be done. One scholar who has done a great deal to highlight the potential importance of battlefield archaeology to our understanding of ancient warfare and more is Jo Ball. Battlefield archaeology emphasizes all those little pieces usually passed over in the aftermath of battle.[3] While bodies and equipment are likely to have been retrieved afterwards because of the value of weapons and armour to both the winning and losing side and the perceived importance of burying the dead, there were usually plenty of little things that would get missed. This would include personal items (broaches, rings, etc.) and little projectiles (lead bullets, arrowheads, etc.). This sort of material might seem incidental to combat, but this sort of approach has been pivotal to our understanding of the Battle of Baecula and the Varus disaster, which I touched on in the introduction. But let's look at some other examples.

In her recent PhD thesis, Ball includes all sorts of interesting material about combat archaeology in the ancient Mediterranean, and some of her discussion touches on the Punic Wars. Here are some highlights.[4] Besides the two sites mentioned above, Ball highlights important work at La Lantejuela, which has been identified with the battles at Munda, one of which was fought in the Second Punic War.[5] There have been some exciting excavations off the coast of southern Italy, which have illuminated aspects of the earlier First Punic War. Our understanding of the Battle of Egadi, which came near the end of the first war, has been transformed by these excavations. This battle, Rome's final naval victory, came off the coast of the Aegates islands as they were known (Egadi Islands today) on 10 March, 241 BCE. The battle is discussed by Polybius.[6] The evidence of the excavations, much of it comprising ships' rams but also things like Montefortino helmets, is not quite in line with what Polybius reported: he claimed the battle was fought entirely involving quinqueremes, while the remains of the ships reveal the presence of triremes.[7]

Another battle that has benefitted from sustained excavation is Baecula, fought in Spain in 208 BCE. Excavations have revealed the marching camps of the opposing Roman and Carthaginian armies at Cerro de las Albahacas in Spain. Excavators have also found things like assorted weapons, impedimenta (equipment for expeditions), pottery, and more.[8] We have some additional literary sources too, like Plutarch, Diodorus Siculus, and Appian. Most historians, however, put most of their trust in what Polybius had to say.

The established narrative has it that Hasdrubal, the Carthaginian commander, had a garrison at New Carthage, and that he would spend his winter at Tarraco. In the spring of 208 BCE, Hasdrubal had encamped by a river with a ridge at the front. Scipio had been off to intercept the Carthaginian and marched towards him with his army. He was determined to engage him sooner rather than later, for he feared the arrival of Mago and Gisgo. Scipio made camp and left some troops behind to watch things over while he sent some troops, *velites* (light infantry) especially, to fight the Carthaginian army, while some others were sent to block Hasdrubal's potential escape in the valley. The Carthaginians lined up for battle and there was an attack on the ridge of the hill, with the Romans split in two and approaching from both the left and the right. Hasdrubal hadn't expected this, feeling confident in his position. What had been less clear before the important excavations was the exact positions of the two armies and some of the specifics of the course of the encounter. Besides what I noted above, the excavations have enlightened us on the strategic position of the battlefield, its topography, and the relative availability of water. With the help of GIS (Geographic Information System), they've been able to pinpoint some potential troop movements too.

Assuming excavations like this continue, they should help us to understand more about this conflict, even from a sensory perspective. While it might seem to go without saying that taste and smell, as manifested through a need for water, and sight, as manifested through deciding to camp in positions that afforded clear views of the vicinity, might seem obvious, finding archaeological remains that confirm our assumptions is helpful. In the case of this specific battle, Hasdrubal and his Carthaginian force were very well prepared. Their position allowed them to keep track of Roman movements, and it forced the Romans to position themselves in a spot where their view would be obstructed. This meant, if they had to retreat, the Romans would not be able to see them (and so attack). The archaeological evidence from Baecula, then, illuminates an important aspect of the visual experience of battle in this instance.[9] Again, as we turn to the Romans in this chapter, we see that the sources are many and varied, with a great deal of potential for senses in history and warfare.

The Build-Up to Cannae

The Battle of Cannae came early in the Second Punic War, the second of three wars waged between the Romans and Carthaginians. Though Cannae turned into a major Roman defeat, they had already suffered in the run-up to this battle. At Lake Trasimene, for example, the Romans had suffered mightily – so much so that they had declared an ultimate decree of the Senate and proclaimed Quintus Fabius Maximus Verrucosus a dictator, a six-month position which gave the bearer ultimate power over all military forces. Fabius decided to use this position to keep Hannibal at bay: he would shadow the Carthaginian general without engaging him in the field. This move was good for Rome, but bad for Rome's allies, who suffered at Hannibal's hands – and who didn't receive the expected Roman support. Nevertheless, it all seemed to be going well for Fabius until he reached the Falernian Field. There, though he thought he had Hannibal hemmed in, Fabius managed to allow him to escape. Roman unrest over Fabius' tactics grew, and when his term came to an end the Romans sought to bring Hannibal to battle.

In 216 BCE, Rome had two new consuls, Caius Terentius Varro, a plebeian new man (i.e. he was the first of his family to be consul), and Lucius Aemilius Paullus, a patrician from a distinguished family. Varro was eager to engage Hannibal at the first opportunity, while Paullus was much more reserved. Regardless of the intentions of these two consuls, it was the Senate back in Rome ultimately pulling the strings.

Despite Hannibal's victory, however, all wasn't well with the Carthaginian army. He struggled to win Roman allies over to his side (some had switched sides, others hadn't), and as he continued he started to run low on supplies, especially when he had to try to keep away from Roman armies in pursuit. So, Hannibal soon decided that he had to force the Romans to engage him in a big battle, and by the summer of 216 BCE he had made it to Cannae, a town in southern Italy that had been razed. Here, Hannibal set up shop, largely because there were good supplies all round, with which he could keep his army operational. This concerned the Romans, who went off to engage the general.

At this stage of the war, the two armies were quite different. The Romans had a relatively new batch of recruits, while the Carthaginian army was full of seasoned veterans, well experienced with warfare on the Italian peninsula. But the Romans decided to send a bigger-than-normal army with larger-than-normal legions. Traditionally, at this stage of Roman history, a legion would number about 4,000 men, but these legions each numbered about 5,000.[10] What is more, there were more of the manipular legions. The manipular legion used comprised the following parts: *velites*, *hastati*, *principes*, and *triarii*, with each type of soldier having a particular place in the battle line.

Primarily, the legion was infantry, with the ratio usually about fourteen infantrymen to every cavalryman. While the numbers seemed to be an advantage, the terrain at Cannae seemed to favour cavalry, which gave Hannibal an advantage. The Carthaginian cavalry outnumbered that of their Roman opponents, with more than 10,000 horsemen (of diverse origins, though Numidian especially) present at the battle, perhaps twice as many (if not more) than the Romans. Overall there might have been as many as 65,000 to 80,000 Roman soldiers at Cannae, and perhaps 45,000 for the Carthaginians.[11]

When the two sides had arrived at Cannae and set up camp, preparations began for battle. As noted, the senate was pulling the strings, even if the command of the Roman armies should be in the hands of the elected consuls. Delays in communications borne by limitations in the technology, however, meant that the consuls were able to act on their own, at least to some degree. It was Hannibal who offered battle first. Paullus wasn't interested, while Varro was. Ordinarily, at this point two consuls with *imperium* (the right to lead an army) wouldn't have been deployed in the same spot, but these circumstances were exceptional. This did make for some potential complications regarding who had the greater authority, and to fix this the two consuls alternated supreme commands on different days. That means that when Hannibal offered battle and Paullus said no, the next day, when he was in charge, Varro could come back and say yes, which he did. And so on 2 August, 216 BCE, the two armies lined up for battle.

There were some significant environmental features to this battle. The Aufidus River on one side served as a restriction to free movement, while mountains surrounded the plain in which the battle was fought (see Images 13 and 14). The Romans chose this spot with the view to using the Aufidus to their advantage. It didn't work out as they hoped, however.

The opening stages were full of sensory stimuli including, potentially, naked Celts on the Carthaginian side, and screaming combatants on both sides. The Balearic slingers, again on Hannibal's side, opened up the engagement and sent missiles whistling towards the Romans. Paullus was even struck by a sling shot.[12] As the two sides engaged, the Romans managed to push the Carthaginians back, while the

Numidians, on the Carthaginian side, managed to push back Varro and the Italians. Indeed, it should be noted that allied armies played a big part in this battle and the wider war. Anyway, thanks to Varro's withdrawal with the Italians, the Roman cavalry were destroyed, which put the larger Roman force in a bit of a bind.

The bombardment of Roman forces by the Carthaginians was nearly constant.[13] The battle stress on the participants was significant, and in the melee the majority of the Romans were trapped. Hannibal and the centre of the Carthaginian line, who had a staggered formation, withdrew, so enticing the Romans opposite in pursuit. But the Carthaginian forces had planned this all along, sucking the Romans into a trap. After the Romans had pushed through in the centre, the Carthaginian line formed a crescent and its wings worked to encircle the Roman forces. Before long the Romans were trapped, and the slaughter began. By some reckoning, it was the bloodiest battle in antiquity. Paullus and another leading figure, Minucius, died, while Varro survived. As for the regular soldiers, Roman casualties might have numbered as high as 50,000, and a number of the survivors became Carthaginian prisoners of war.

Not surprisingly, the battle's outcome has engendered a great deal of debate, both then and now, with Polybius favouring a tactical explanation, which includes a consideration of the relative merits of infantry versus cavalry, and the role of Hannibal's leadership. Livy's explanation hints at a role for the divine and some tactical issues. The Romans might have explained their defeat in terms of flaws in how they performed rituals, and they might even trace it to a violation of religious law. By some ancient reckoning, the Romans were even fated to lose this battle.[14] Modern explanations have stressed the failure of Roman cavalry or the confined space of the battlefield. Leadership too has been flagged, with the Roman leaders pale versions of their Carthaginian peer. The deficiencies of the Romans troops, who, as noted, had much less experience than the Carthaginians with as many as two-thirds new recruits, have also been flagged. Then there are some of the more common issues that befall defeated armies, like panic and the concomitant loss of organization that usually goes with it.

Regardless of the explanation, that it was a major loss for Rome is certain. As I've said too, it's also been the subject of quite a lot of research. It's time to shift to the senses to bring out more of the lived experience of the battle.

Seeing

The basic components of the Roman mid-republican battle line are well-established (see Image 15). The *velites* stood at the front, but moved to the back as the battle progressed.[15] The *hastati*, the youngest of the three central groups of legionaries, stood near the front of the line, and faced the enemy once the *velites* pulled back. The *principes*, the mid-ranking legionaries, followed the *hastati* and stood in the middle. At the rear you'd find the *triarii*, the most experienced of the lot. Cavalry would be at each side of the Roman legion. The allies, it is said, had a similar organization, at least so far as we know, and could be found anywhere along the line.[16] While we know the general parts of this Roman chequerboard formation, the *quincunx*, we're less clear about why the different groups (which were based on age) were positioned where they were. The usual thinking is that the *hastati*, who might have made up two fifths of the total, did the bulk of the fighting, with the rear lines replacing the frontal ones as needed. Once they'd had enough, the *principes* would pick up the slack. If worst came to worst, the *triarii* would finally get involved. This method does make a great deal of sense when we consider the age of the different groups. When I was 19, the age of a *hastatus*, I could run for miles. Twenty years later, I'm lucky if I can manage a few feet. The youngest men could, in theory, hold out the longest in a prolonged battle. It would also mean employing the trial-by-fire experience technique.

That said, the placing of the least experienced men at the front makes sense from the perspective of sight too. Battle was a confusing, chaotic, and disorientating thing.[17] Smith regularly comments on the disorientation felt by the greenest troops in the Civil War.[18] The unease felt by the most inexperienced of American soldiers would have matched that of Roman soldiers. To ease the transition, it would make a great deal of sense to give those with the least familiarity with battle the clearest view of what was transpiring, and in a Roman battle formation this would be those deployed at the front. Polybius himself commented on how few of the soldiers at Cannae would have seen what they were up against before.[19] If you'd already lived through countless battles, you'd be less likely to be traumatized by all those things that you could hear, smell, touch, and even taste, but not see. Even if the *triarii* couldn't see what was transpiring, there's good reason to suppose they had a good idea what was happening. Placing the least experienced at the front gave them the best opportunity to overcome their fears by giving them the clearest view. Those who don't need to see, are best placed at the back. Additionally, Asclepiodotus and Xenophon, albeit discussing a different context, say that the most experienced soldiers were often placed at the back of military formations to prevent the less experienced from fleeing.[20]

Considering the experience of the commanders and the cavalry provides insight into how access to sight might have been closely controlled. It also might help to explain the general character of most ancient battle descriptions. By the end of the third century BCE, the heroic mode of generalship – generalship in the vein of Alexander the Great – had fallen out of fashion, in part due to the vast numbers of men involved in most ancient battles. This was largely true of Rome too, despite any lingering desires for displays of *virtus* (manly courage).[21] Ideally, the commander would manage his troops rather than take a stand in amongst the ranks. Indeed, Paullus was deployed on the right with the Roman cavalry, while Varro was deployed on the left, in his case with Rome's allied cavalry.[22] From these vantage points, the consuls could see much more of what was happening than their lower-ranking fellow soldiers in the heart of the Roman formation. The desire for a bird's-eye view in most ancient accounts of battle might be a reflection of the social position of a text's audience: members of the elite whose military experience, if they had much of it, would have been as battle-managing commanders.[23] The importance of sight to the commanders – the most privileged participants in a battle like this – is evident in other aspects too. Military manuals, though many extant ones post-date this battle, focus on how the eyes can mislead, or how you can use tricks to mislead your foes' eyes. If you don't have enough men, for instance, they describe how to make it look like you have more than you do.[24] Polybius was himself a general, and he regularly emphasizes the importance of vision to the commanders whom he describes, who in turn often stress its role to their men, like Paullus and Hannibal do before Cannae.[25]

Other topics we could have mentioned include the role sight plays in mid-battle communications. In mid-battle, words were meaningless, but a standard could be invaluable. While battle was raging it could be difficult to hear the orders of commanders. To counter this, the Romans used their standards to help communicate manoeuvres (where possible) to the men. A standard could provide a highly visible mark for orientation and a rallying point. In this case, the use of sight could help overcome the deficiencies in sound. There's also the wind: Livy says the Volturnus wind blew in the face of the Roman soldiers during the battle:

> Near that village Hannibal had pitched camp, facing away from the Volturnus wind, which blows clouds of dust over the dry, torrid plains…the Carthaginians…would be facing away from the wind, which would be only at their backs, and they would be fighting an enemy half-blinded by clouds of dust.[26]

If Livy was right, and the wind was blowing dust in the eyes of the Roman soldiers, this would have had a significant impact on the battle's course. Incidentally, the conditions at Trebia also had a severe impact on the vision of Rome's army.[27] There's also, of course, the traumatizing impact of the spectacle of the fallen. The sight of many tens of thousands wounded, dying, and dead men and animals is likely to have left a lasting mark on the survivors of the battle.

Hearing

From sight we move to sound. In his account of the bombardment of Fort Sumter in Charleston harbour, Smith describes the varied soundscape. On the one hand, there was the chatter amongst the free and the enslaved of the city; on the other, the booming sounds of the cannon balls fired towards, and crashing into, the fort. While a battle in a plain like Cannae is not the same thing as a bombardment of a fort in a city, it too had a mixed soundscape.

There were no cannon or *ballistae* at Cannae. Indeed, the Romans seemed to have eschewed artillery in pitched battles in this period (though not in later eras), so we wouldn't get the sounds of missiles being fired from large machines. That being said, we do know that slingers played a significant role in the battle. The Carthaginians, for instance, deployed Balearic slingers in their army, arguably the most-famed slingers of the ancient world. Paullus himself was famously struck by one.[28] While bullets and slings might seem some of the least threatening weapons of ancient battles, those bullets could be slung by experienced slingers at speeds approaching 100mph. Not only could they inflict physical damage, but they could also dish out psychological damage. Some of the bullets that have been recovered around the world contained not just the juvenile insults of war-hardened soldiers, but little holes whose original purpose was unclear. Fairly recent research, admittedly concerned with bullets recovered in Scotland, revealed that those holes caused the bullets to whistle as they flew through the air.[29] While we don't know what sorts of bullets were used at Cannae, if they contained these little holes, we can well imagine that the sound of hundreds, even thousands, of flying bullets would make for a terrifying experience.[30] Cannon balls they were not, but perhaps no less intimidating.

At the start of the Second Punic War, Polybius claims that the Romans and their allies could supply about 700,000 infantry soldiers and 70,000 cavalry.[31] While the largest proportion were Roman, sizeable contributions were made by Cenomani, Etruscans, Sabines, Sarsinates, Umbrians, and Veneti, among others. The predominant language of the Roman army would have been Latin; but given that nearly half its members were from allied contingents that's not the only language you would have heard coming from the Roman side. During idle moments, and in the heat of battle, you were likely to have heard a cacophony of voices speaking if not many languages, at least a few. This would have been no less true of the Carthaginians, however, for their army was at least as polyglot, with troop contingents comprising

Celtiberians, Gauls, Libyans, Numidians and more. Our sources present the pre-battle speeches of some generals, including Paullus and Hannibal, though as we well know they are unlikely to have gone quite as described, not with the kinds of numbers involved in the battle – many tens of thousands.[32] Still, some sort of pre-battle words seem likely, and given the highest-ranking commanders were Roman they would have been in Latin. Just like the well-known later incident of the soldier and the ass from Apuleius' *Metamorphoses*, the language of power in the army was Latin.[33]

In the first chapter, I talked a bit about Greek and Persian war cries. Unsurprisingly, all sorts of peoples had war cries of their own, with Livy and Polybius drawing attention to those of the Gauls, and Tacitus to that of the Britons.[34] Well, the Romans and Carthaginians – and their assorted allies – had cries of their own. Unsurprisingly, in the case of Carthage we have to rely on the Roman evidence, which isn't always forthcoming. Livy, one of our best sources for Punic War matters, doesn't give us specifics about many Carthaginian things, their war cry included. He does say, however, that it left its mark on unfamiliar Romans. At the Battle of the River Ticinus, the sound of it drove the Romans in flight. Livy says: 'scarcely had the battle shout been raised before the javelin men retired to the second line among the reserves'.[35] A book later, Livy reports that the sounds of the Carthaginians combined with the Romans' limited visibility to wreak havoc on their battleline:

> The shout of the battle rose round the Romans before they could see clearly from whence it came, or became aware that they were surrounded. Fighting began in front and flank before they could form line or get their weapons ready or draw their swords.[36]

In all of the cases where Livy touches on the impact of Carthage's war cry on the Romans, the only instance where it didn't have a marked impact was the Battle of Zama, the famous one in which Scipio Africanus defeated Hannibal, so ending the war.[37] Polybius describes it too, but he doesn't add any specifics, instead noting:

When they came withing distance the Roman soldiers charged the
enemy, shouting as usual their war cry...while the Carthaginian
mercenaries uttered a strange confusion of cries, the effect of
which was indescribable.[38]

As for the Roman version, it obviously went through many changes as
the empire expanded and its military became more diverse. According
to Dionysius of Halicarnassus, a big part of the Roman battle cry in
the republican era was the trumpet, which would sound the charge.
It would be followed by the cry itself, which he didn't differentiate.[39]
Sometimes this cry was just shouting, or so Plutarch says.[40] Indeed,
both Cassius Dio and Josephus talk about the piercing shout of Roman
cries from the late republic and early imperial eras.[41] We don't actually
get much in the way of specifics about the Roman cry until the late
empire, when both Ammianus Marcellinus and Vegetius talk a bit
about the then Roman *barritus*, a point to which we will return in
Chapter 5.[42]

To get back to the other sounds of combat, the chaos of battle could
nullify the role of language, for when it came to the heat of battle, Latin
commands would likely have been inaudible to most soldiers, and so to
communicate, besides making full use of their standards, the Romans
regularly relied on musical instruments. From this perspective, the
most important sound wasn't the spoken language the Romans used,
but the musical one. There were three instruments used regularly by
Roman republican armies, the *tuba*, the *cornu*, and the *buccina*.[43] These
instruments might be used for all sorts of things in peacetime, like
the changing of the guard during the night watch,[44] or to summon
the soldiers together.[45] When it came to battle, the instruments were
used to signal the movement of soldiers, the start of battle, or even
a retreat.[46] Sometimes too the sounds of the instruments worked in
conjunction with the motions of the *signum*: together they could signal
a whole array of movements and orders in the heat of battle, at least in
theory.[47] Ultimately, the confusion of battle had the ability to nullify
the power of Latin and bring many soldiers to the same level.

Touching

What about touch? While there were any number of potential tactile experiences in a pitched battle like Cannae, from the feel of a weapon to the weight of the armour, the one that I want to focus on here is the touching of man against man in the compression of an ancient battle formation. As we've seen in the previous chapters, a big part of any battle was the respective formations of the two sides, themselves composed of masses of men in individual battle lines of varied breadth and depth. Owing to the literary intentions of most Greek and Roman authors (literary colour at the expense of tactical and organizational detail), the specifics of those formations (how many men per line and their spacing) is a matter of debate. What we can say, however, is that the tactile experience of a battle formation would have had an impact on those involved, and it would have changed depending on the circumstances.

Much Roman tactical debate surrounds the spacing between members in a formation.[48] The sources aren't precise enough, which leaves a lot of uncertainty, and there's unlikely to be consensus any time soon. Whether there were three feet separating soldiers in a Roman line or six feet, Cannae posed significant challenges.[49] With the River Aufidus marking one boundary, the space was much more restrictive than usual for the Roman army, and this would later come to haunt them. The Roman cavalry wasn't able to engage in some of the wheeling and turning that they usually could.[50] Hannibal seems to have planned to envelop the Romans and their allies before the battle even started. His careful deployment of his forces led to a weakening of his own centre at the start – it gave way and the Roman infantry pushed through. Eventually, however, the Carthaginian forces on the flanks, which had been successful, wheeled inwards to envelop a huge proportion of the Roman army including most if not all of their infantry.[51] As such, the Romans were soon hemmed into a confined space. What would have made matters worse was the tendency, argued by some, for soldiers to crowd together in times of danger.[52] By all accounts, they no longer had enough space to wield their weapons effectively, and the Carthaginians started to pick them off. As it happens, however, the Roman cavalry ran into a similar problem, as Livy notes:

hemmed in by the river on one side, and by the lines of infantry on the other...horses came to a standstill, and were then crowded together in a mass, rider grappled with rider, each trying to drag the other from his mount.[53]

This is all eerily reminiscent of the Teutoburg Forest, and as we saw in the introduction, it didn't go well for Varus and the Romans there. In this earlier instance, which came at the beginning of the battle, the Romans had managed to push back the Carthaginian cavalry. In the latter episode, however, not only could the infantry not see what was going on, but they couldn't move either. Most perished where they stood: they weren't able to escape, boxed in by the closeness of their friends and foes. By and large, the Roman casualties were heaped up over just a few square miles.

The tactile crush of a battle like Cannae is not just about the sensory experience, however, for it reveals something about power relations, both between the two sides and even within Rome. The more powerful groups in battle invariably had greater room to move. As a result of its successes, the Carthaginian army could move around freely, at least to a point, which prevented the problem of them getting pushed up against their comrades like the Romans did.[54] Even on the Roman side, the more powerful often had greater freedom of movement – and could retire so they wouldn't be crushed up against their comrades.

As noted, most of the Roman soldiers who died in the battle perished where they stood.[55] Not only was this true for thousands of regular soldiers, but even some high-ranking ones too. The previous year's consuls both died in this way, though they are said to have fought bravely.[56] One of the current consuls, Varro, escaped, while the other, Paullus, perished. It is with these two that we see some of the advantages that their position afforded. One of the main reasons why Varro was able to escape was his privileged position on one of the flanks and his riding of a horse: this made it much easier for him to get out of any potentially tight spot. Paullus, though he died, didn't die where he fell like so many others. In fact, we don't know the exact circumstances of his death, though we do know that he was able to take a break from the fighting at one point to stop and sit on a rock, where he was noticed by Lentulus, one of the tribunes, as he was fleeing.[57] Paullus' privileged position meant that he didn't need to worry about being pressed up against his peers. None of his lower-ranking soldiers would have been able to pause and contemplate life in the middle of battle quite like he did.

On the one hand, the heat of battle could be the great leveller, for all of those caught in the melee would be exposed to the same closeness and crush of their comrades, whether lowly *hastatus* or high-ranking pro-magistrate. On the other hand, the experiences of Paullus reveal that power did have its perks, even if, in the end, he did meet his fate.

Senses at Cannae: Some Highlights

A significant component of American Civil War battles was the use of guns. Their impact was so pronounced that the phrase, 'smelling the powder' came to be used as a shorthand amongst the soldiers for fighting.[58] While there is, so far as I know, no comparable phrase from the Roman world, there are still some potential parallels between the two wars. The number of casualties from the Battle of Gettysburg was not unlike the total from Cannae.[59] Just as the battlefield at Gettysburg would have been littered with the swelling corpses of men and horses, so too would this have been the case at Cannae.[60] If Polybius and Livy are right, there might have been as many as 47,700 dead Roman soldiers, and another 2,700 horses, plus however many allied soldiers and their horses.[61] The smell of the decomposing bodies at Gettysburg wouldn't have been unlike that at Cannae, for not only did both battles result in a remarkable number of casualties, but both were fought in hot conditions. At Gettysburg, bodies began decomposing within twenty-four hours and the stench would have been horrible.[62] The average daily high in the region of Cannae in August today is about 33°C, and there's no reason to think that 2 August 216 BCE, wasn't a hot day. And this is to say nothing about how the odour of thousands of sweaty men, some of whom must have urinated or defecated, contributed to all of this. In short, the smell would have been powerful, and it helps us to understand, at least in part, why the Romans chose to burn their war dead where they lay on the field of battle. There might well have been all sorts of cultural and religious reasons; but there's also no doubt that there were all sorts of practical reasons too, at least in those battles where this was possible.

A key role for taste was implied in my grandiloquent opening. The reason why Cannae was chosen as a battlefield in the first place was its housing of some key Roman storage facilities. For all Hannibal's success in the war to this point, the general was running low on supplies and keen to find more grain for his men. Forage and plunder only got you so far, and southern Italy, though the home of some Carthaginian allies, was full of plenty of Carthaginian foes too.[63] Thus, securing a ready source of grain would have enabled him to keep his army fed and in the field. Conversely, from the Roman perspective, Cannae had served as one of their key sources of supplies in this part of Italy. Just as gaining it would give Hannibal a boost, its loss would put the Romans at a disadvantage.

In the Battle of Baecula, noted at the beginning of this chapter, which pitted Scipio Africanus against Hasdrubal Barca, some of the significant finds included items pertaining to the two marching camps. Besides those excavations, we also have some scattered evidence from what remains of Polybius, and a little more from Livy. By Livy's account, the Romans won handily; he also notes Hasdrubal's escape before the battle was over. He collected a bunch of supplies and then marched off towards the Pyrenees. When Scipio and the Romans made it to the camp after it was over, he allowed the Carthaginians to round up some booty.[64] Although Livy doesn't specifically mention things to eat and drink, it likely played a part in the aftermath. To follow the famous maxim usually attributed either to Napoleon or Frederick the Great, an army really did march on its stomach, which attention to the taste of battle brings out.

Hunger, of course, is not exactly the same thing as taste, though the two are not unrelated. Both sides, especially as the battle dragged on, might have been eager to taste some fresh food and drink to recharge. Both Hanson and Keegan have noted the propensity of some armies to have booze before battle.[65] As it happens, there are references to Romans and others doing the same, at least in some circumstances and some decades after Cannae.[66] In the thick of battle, however, it is likely other things would have crossed their lips. As note above, the Battle of Cannae was fought on a hot, dry day, and so it follows that the soldiers on both sides would have tasted the dust of the surrounding plain, though the Romans in particular, given that the wind was blowing towards them. It's likely too that they would have tasted blood, both their own and that of their opponents, neither of which is a particularly pleasant prospect. Piercing wounds to the stomach and any sharp or blunt force blows to the mouth or jaw could cause soldiers to taste blood. A serious stab wound to the lungs might also cause a soldier to cough up, and so taste, blood.[67] Although he doesn't describe the taste of blood, Livy does say this:

> Some, covered with blood, raised themselves from among the dead around them, tortured by their wounds which were nipped by the cold of the morning, and were promptly put an end to by the enemy. Some they found lying with their thighs and knees gashed but still alive; these bared their throats and necks and bade them drain what blood they still had left.[68]

Other potential tastes include water, tears and soil. We don't hear about any soldiers plunging into the neighbouring river once the battle turns and the Romans try to escape, though Livy, at least, notes it provided a fresh source of water at its start.[69] By the time the battle was over, however, the river's waters ran red with blood.[70] At the earlier Battle of Lake Trasimene, the water sometimes came up to the soldiers' shoulders, and it seems inevitable that in the melee many would have tasted, even choked on, water.[71] Tears, of course, are mostly water, and likely tears were shed (and tasted) in the fighting at Cannae, especially in the aftermath as soldiers mourned their fallen comrades.[72] Some even swallowed dirt, if Livy is to be believed, for they preferred suffocation by burying their heads in the ground to death at the hands of the Carthaginians:

> Some were discovered with their heads buried in the earth, they had evidently suffocated themselves by making holes in the ground and heaping soil on their faces.[73]

Postscript: New Carthage

Before I close, I want to stress that for all the horror wrought on Rome in this battle by Carthage, they were equally capable of doing the same the other way. I also want to set the scene for siege warfare, the topic of the next chapter. To do all this, I want to finish by saying a few things about the siege of New Carthage that took place in the latter half of the war in 209 BCE in Spain. New Carthage was key to Carthage's position in Spain. The site was naturally well defended with a large civilian population and a small garrison. Though the city was important, they hadn't expected a Roman attack. The Roman army, under Scipio, comprised 25,000 infantry, 2,500 cavalry, and a fleet. When the assault began, it was on the landward side, and a Roman fleet encircled the city. In charge of the defence was Mago, who split the city's 1,000-strong garrison and armed 2,000 civilians.

When the attack came, there were plenty of skirmishes outside the city's walls, with the Romans' numerical superiority usually working to their advantage. Sometimes the Romans tried bringing ladders up to the walls with a view to scaling them, but their height prevented the Romans from making much progress (see Image 16). Usually, walls could serve as a mild deterrent to certain siege tactics. Practically they had value as well. Fortunately for Rome and unfortunately for Carthage, Scipio knew a great deal about the city, including the defensive weakness of its lagoon and its changing water levels, both details which Scipio used to his benefit. Attacks continued along the city's walls with ladders, and while this was going on other large groups of soldiers crossed the lagoon as its waters receded. Eventually, Scipio and the Romans entered the city, and the general famously sent out his soldiers to slaughter the inhabitants, but in what's been characterized (somewhat dubiously) as a controlled way. Polybius' description is gruesome:

> When Scipio thought that a sufficient number of troops had entered he sent most of them, as is the Roman custom, against the inhabitants of the city with orders to kill all they encountered, sparing none, and not to start pillaging until the signal was given.

They do this, I think, to inspire terror, so that when towns are taken by the Romans one may often see not only the corpses of human beings, but dogs cut in half, and the dismembered limbs of other animals, and on this occasion such scenes were very many owing to the numbers of those in the place.[74]

Mago, meanwhile, begged for his life. Once the slaughter ended, the looting began, with the equipment haul itself spectacular.[75] To highlight some key sensory aspects, the pivotal moments, when the Romans were on the verge of taking the city, were filled with panicked shouting by the defenders.[76] The chaotic soundscape filled with desperate and maddened voices would have been a distinctive feature. On the Roman side, their communications, still largely audible, were controlled, at least in Polybius' telling, though the reality might have been different. Still, he says, for instance, that when night fell and Scipio took a position on New Carthage's citadel, he communicated to his men by means of his tribunes, whom he ordered to collect the booty and guard it.[77] Messengers were an effective means of communicating in loud environments. When it came to collecting booty, Scipio ordered half the men to go about the city gathering what they could, while the rest would stand firm and guard their activities. The sight of all these Roman soldiers, some perhaps a bit crazed, some with incomprehensible order, would likely have brought fear in equal measure to assembled masses. That said, Polybius claims that Scipio treated the inhabitants with considerable leniency and mercy, so the inhabitants' experiences might not have been as bad as they might otherwise have been.

The relative speed of this siege meant that tasting and smelling might have been less pronounced for the defenders – and the attackers – than it might otherwise have been. Though that's not to say they wouldn't have experienced some hardships, the defenders at least, while all this was unfolding. In the next chapter, this sort of scene, a Roman siege of a town or city, is the subject, with sensory experience of those on the receiving of the siege of a city the particular focus.

Chapter 4

The Sieges of Jerusalem (70 CE) and Masada (72–74 CE)

O ne of the conflicts from the Roman world about which we are well informed is the Jewish War waged between the Romans and the Jews or Judaeans in the first century, between 66 and 73/74 CE. It is a war about which we know a great deal thanks to the detailed account given by Flavius Josephus, who started the war on the side of the rebels, but who finished it on the side of the Romans. In this chapter, after providing an overview of our sources and a quick run-down of the war, I'll turn to the sieges of Jerusalem and then Masada to look closer at what an emphasis on a sensory approach to these sieges can tell us about the experiences of some of their participants.

Sources[1]

We start with the sources. As I said, the most famous and important source for the war is probably Flavius Josephus. He was a member of the priestly class in Judea and a priest himself, who fought on the rebel or Jewish side in the conflict. His service on the Jewish side came to an end at Jotapata (modern Yodfat) during the 47-day siege in 67 CE. At the siege's end, he was captured by the Romans and became a prisoner, but he ended up befriending the Flavians. He worked with the Jews vis-à-vis the Romans in the rest of the conflict, and this included his participation in some negotiations during the famous siege of Jerusalem.

Josephus is only important to us because he wrote about his experiences. Josephus was an active author best known for three works: an autobiography, his *Jewish Antiquities*, and most importantly his *Jewish War*. The *Jewish War* was the first written of those three, compiled just a few years after the war's conclusion. It seemed, however, that he wrote a slightly earlier version, in Aramaic, before turning his hand to the Greek version. Josephus was commissioned to write the *Jewish War*, and acts as an apologist for the Flavians as well as particular groups within the Jewish diaspora, possibly the Pharisees. As a result of this, his reputation is mixed. There are questions too about his works' survival, particularly why his account has and not that of later writers. The consensus seems to be that later Christian readers approved of his interpretation, and so kept it for their own use.[2]

Although Josephus is probably the most important of our sources, he wasn't the only one. Tacitus' *Annals* presumably described the war in detail, though it's now lost. Fortunately, there have been extensive excavations of important sites connected to the war in Israel. Coinage connected to the war – minted in celebration from a Roman perspective – has been unearthed. Archaeologists have made important discoveries at places like Gamla, Jerusalem, and Masada. In the case of the former, Gamla, excavators found bolts from *ballistae*, Roman siege machines, and more, including several important weapons. As far as the projectile pieces go, along with some bolts, the excavators found *ballista* balls and arrowheads in the town's ramparts.[3] In other sites, notable finds include the siege works of Masada, including the giant rampart constructed by the Romans, to the occasional body, including the young woman who perished in Jerusalem's burnt house.

Collectively, this diverse body of evidence affords us a far more detailed understanding of the war and its course than for many other conflicts from the ancient world. Indeed, the literary record from Josephus combined with the material finds from Jerusalem and Masada give us nearly unprecedented insight into siege warfare during the Roman era, though the siege of Dura Europos, to which we'll turn in Chapter 6, gives it a good run for its money.

The Jewish War: An Overview[4]

As for the war itself, there had been hostility between the diverse residents of the region in the decades leading up to its outbreak. Assorted Roman officials had done a poor job of integrating the conquered people into local culture, admittedly a problem across the empire. But some of the problems were particularly pronounced in Judea owing, in part, to Roman bafflement in the face of Jewish religious practices (the monotheistic tendencies) and beyond. Sometimes these issues started right at the top. Gaius Caesar (r. 37–41 CE), better known as Caligula, tried to make the Great Temple in Jerusalem a home to the imperial cult, one of the most important religious bodies in the Roman world. There were temples to the imperial cult across the empire, where elites and regular Romans empire-wide would perform rituals for the health and wellbeing of the emperor and his family. The Jews, however, had been exempt from participating in the rituals associated with the imperial cult.

Caligula's successor, Claudius (r. 41–54 CE), appointed Herod Agrippa I (r. 37–44 CE) king of Judea. Under his tutelage, Judea witnessed a major construction boom coupled with the expansion of the kingdom's territory. Upon his death, however, his son wasn't appointed as successor. Instead, the kingdom was put under the administration of Syria. By the 60s CE, two Roman administrators, Lucceius Albinus (62–64 CE) and Gessius Florus (64–66 CE), were famed for their greed and cruelty. Procurators ran territories that fell somewhere between client kingdoms and provinces, and there were seven in Judea before it became a province. Needless to say, for a variety of reasons, Judea was ripe for conflagration.

One long term problem had been the presence of *sicarii*, bandits. Additionally, on the coast in Caesarea, there was trouble concerning access to the temple, which was obstructed to a large degree by private properties owned by gentiles. As worshippers passed by these neighbouring properties on their way to the temple, they would be mocked by pagans and gentiles alike. There were attempts to smooth things over by Agrippa II and Berenice, but they failed. The last straw was the seizure of money from the Temple in Jerusalem by the procurator Florus. After a brief period of disquiet among the local populace, Florus sent in some Roman soldiers to stamp out a would-be insurrection. And just like that, war broke out.

In Jerusalem, insurgents under a certain Menahem took the Upper City; moreover, they massacred a Roman cohort and a high priest. Not all residents supported Menahem, however, for Eleazar, the captain of the temple, executed him and his followers. As a result, Cestius Gallus, the legate from Syria, a heavily militarized neighbouring province, attacked the city and then pulled back, having achieved only limited results. On his way back to Syria, Cestius and his army were defeated at Beth Horon in 66 CE, somewhat unexpectedly. This Jewish attack led to all-out war. Then Emperor Nero, who happened to be in Greece when much of this took place, sent Vespasian and his son Titus in response.

The Roman army under Vespasian made its way through Judea heading south, and the majority of the Jewish forces they encountered fled without a fight. Josephus, the primary literary source for the conflict whom I mentioned above, was captured at Jotapata, where he had been defending the city with a local garrison. Although he started the war on the Jewish side, over the course of his captivity he befriended the Flavians, so starting a relationship which led to later accusations that he was an apologist for Titus and the Romans.

Meanwhile, the Romans, who had made Caesarea and Scythopolis their bases, continued south to Taricheae, the home of Mary Magdalen, and in the process bypassed Jerusalem. The Romans were ruthless in their attacks, though several places, like Gamla, managed to hold out, at least for a time. By 67 CE, Jerusalem was full of refugees and extremists (at least from a Roman perspective) were in charge. Over the course of the war, Vespasian had managed to isolate Judea. When unrest broke out back in Rome with the forced suicide of Nero in 68 CE, Vespasian raced west with an army to take the throne (he succeeded), and he left his elder son Titus in charge.

By 70 CE, Titus and his Roman army had arrived at Jerusalem, and several months later the city was taken, all but ending the war. Victory in the war was celebrated in a grand way back in Rome. There was a triumphal parade, which Josephus describes and which is depicted on Titus' triumphal arch (see Image 17). Josephus' account of the parade is detailed. Here's one especially vivid segment:

> But for those that were taken in the temple of Jerusalem, they made the greatest figure of them all; that is, the golden table, of the weight of many talents; the candlestick also, that was made of

gold, though its construction was now changed from that which we made use of; for its middle shaft was fixed upon a basis, and the small branches were produced out of it to a great length, having the likeness of a trident in their position, and had every one a socket made of brass for a lamp at the tops of them. These lamps were in number seven, and represented the dignity of the number seven among the Jews; and the last of all the spoils, was carried the Law of the Jews. After these spoils passed by a great many men, carrying the images of Victory, whose structure was entirely either of ivory or of gold. After which Vespasian marched in the first place, and Titus followed him; Domitian also rode along with them, and made a glorious appearance, and rode on a horse that was worthy of admiration.[5]

As memorable an occasion as the parade would have been, perhaps the biggest physical vestige of Rome's victory in the war is the Flavian Amphitheatre, or Colosseum, said to have been built using funds acquired in the war.

Jerusalem[6]

The siege of Masada may have come at the end of the war and so represented the final military encounter, but it was the siege of Jerusalem in 70 CE, a carefully thought out and executed attack, that brought the war to its conclusion. From the perspective of the civilians who had to live through the siege, three of the senses are particularly well documented, at least from the perspective of ancient Mediterranean history. The first two are related, taste and smell. Just as the success of an army is dependent on the ability of its leaders to feed the soldiers, so too is the successful withstanding of a siege dependent on the ability of the defenders to feed a city's residents. If a city cannot feed its people, it won't hold out for long. Related to taste, of course, is smell, and as we'll see, the smell of burning flesh gave away an unspeakable act borne out by taste. After that, we come to touch, and how it can be experienced in two different ways.

Before we get to the siege, let's turn back to the middle of the war. At that point, the city was divided, with John of Gischala and some rebels in command of the outer court of the temple and part of the city of David; Eleazar ben Simon and his followers in the inner court of the temple; and Simon bar Giora the Upper City and part of the city of David. Tacitus describes it well:

> The population at this time had been increased by streams of rabble that flowed in from the other captured cities, for the most desperate rebels had taken refuge here, and consequently sedition was the more rife. There were three generals, three armies: the outermost and largest circuit of the walls was held by Simon, the middle of the city by John, and the temple was guarded by Eleazar. John and Simon were strong in numbers and equipment, Eleazar had the advantage of position: between these three there was constant fighting, treachery, and arson, and a great store of grain was consumed. Then John got possession of the temple by sending a party, under pretence of offering sacrifice, to slay Eleazar and his troops. So the citizens were divided into two factions until, at the approach of the Romans, foreign war produced concord.[7]

These divisions meant the city lacked a unified strategy in its defence against the Roman aggressors. What's more, it probably compounded some of the logistical challenges Jerusalem faced. To make matters worse, as we've seen, the Romans purposely avoided Jerusalem, the heart of the insurrection, until they had overcome nearly every rebellious settlement, with Masada the last to hold out. After they'd managed this, Titus and his army arrived in the region in April or May of 70 CE, just as the spring harvest was ready, a deliberate choice. They set up a camp at Mount Scopus and the Mount of Olives, which cut off the city from its food supplies outside of the walls. One of the Romans' principal aims was clearly to starve out the inhabitants. Josephus describes in detail the lengths to which the residents went to satiate their growing hunger.

1. Epitaph of Marcus Caelius, victim of the Battle of the Teutoburg Forest. (*Copyright Agnete, Wikimedia Commons*)

2. Achaemenid Persian Fort, Tall-e Takht, Pasargadae, Iran. The Persians had an extensive fortification network which includes sites like this, part of the Pasargadae World Heritage Site. (*Diego Delso, Wikimedia Commons*)

3. The Battle of Cunaxa fought between the Persians and 10,000 Greek mercenaries of Cyrus the Young, 401 BC, Adrien Guiget, Louvre. (*Copyright Wikimedia Commons*)

4. Hoplite from Dodona Antikensammlung Berlin Misc. 7470. (*Copyright Wikimedia Commons*)

5. The Army of Artaxerxes II on the Tomb of Artaxerxes, Persepolis. The units (ethnic groups) depicted on the top of the frieze, from left to right, are Persian, Median, Elamite, Parthian, Arian, Bactrian, Sogdian, Choresmian, Zarangian, Arachosian, Sattagydian, Gandharan, Hindush, and haumavarga Saka. On the bottom, from left to right, are Makan, tigraxauda Saka, Babylonian, Assyrian, Arab, Egyptian, Armenian, Cappadocian, Lydian, Ionian, overseas Saka, Skudrian, Ionian with shield-hat, Libyan, Ethiopian, and Carian. (*Copyright Adobe Stock*)

6. Battle of Chaironeia, nineteenth century. (*Copyright Wikimedia Commons*)

THE BATTLE-FIELD OF ISSUS.[1]

7. The Battlefield of Issus. (*Copyright Wikimedia Commons*)

8. The location of Issus. (*Copyright Google Earth Pro*)

9. Aerial view of Issus. (*Copyright Google Earth Pro*)

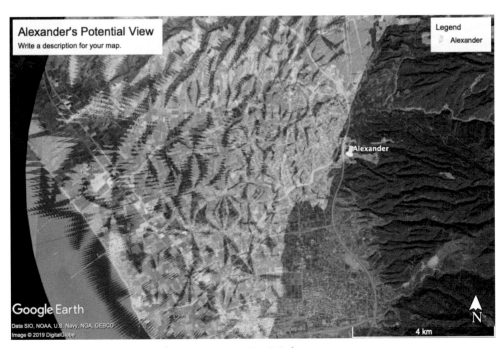

10. Alexander's potential view. (*Copyright Google Earth Pro*)

11. The Alexander Mosaic, from the House of the Faun in Pompeii, Naples Archaeological Museum. (*Copyright Carole Raddato, Wikimedia Commons*)

12. Carthaginian Shekel. The Carthaginians under Hannibal famously marched across the Alps with elephants. (*Wikimedia Commons*)

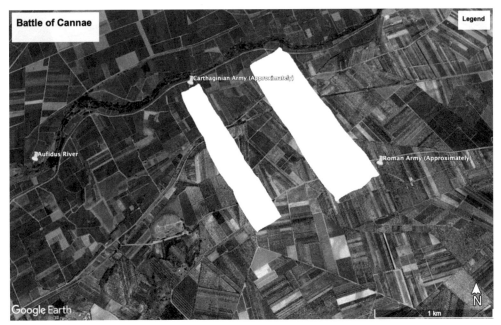

13. Map of area around Cannae. (*Copyright Google Earth Pro*)

14. The modern monument at Cannae. (*Copyright Wikimedia Commons*)

15. Pydna Relief, Monument of Aemilius Paulus. This is our earliest image of a Roman soldier, in sculptural relief, from the middle of the second century BCE. (*Colin Whiting, Wikimedia Commons*)

16. The walls of New Carthage (Cartagena), Spain. (*Copyright Wikimedia Commons*)

17. *Quadriga*, Arch of Titus, Rome. Part of the triumphal parade depicted on the column in sculptural relief. (*Salko, Wikimedia Commons*)

18. Aerial view of Masada. (*Copyright Wikimedia Commons*)

19. The Roman Camp F at Masada. (*Copyright Aren Rozen, Wikimedia Commons*)

20. The Roman ramp at Masada. (*Copyright G Solomon, Wikimedia Commons*)

21. The Cave of Letters. (*Copyright, Israel Antiquities Authority, Wikimedia Commons*)

22. The Black Gate, Trier. (*Copyright Conor Whately*)

23. *Testudo*, Trajan's Column. Though much earlier in date, this is the most famous Roman depiction of a *testudo* that we have. (*Christian Chirita, Wikimedia Commons*)

24. The Roman barracks at el-Lejjūn, Jordan. (*Copyright Conor Whately*)

25. A view of the Rhine from Mainz, Germany. (*Copyright Conor Whately*)

26. The Seizure of Edessa, 1071, in the Chronicle of John Skylitzes. (*Copyright Wikimedia Commons*)

27. Urfa Castle, Urfa/Edessa, Turkey. Some of the most famous extant ruins from Edessa (modern Urfa) are those depicted here, of Abbasid-era Urfa Castle. (*Barnard Gagnon, Wikimedia Commons*)

28. The walls at Diyarbakir, Turkey. (*Copyright Wikimedia Commons*)

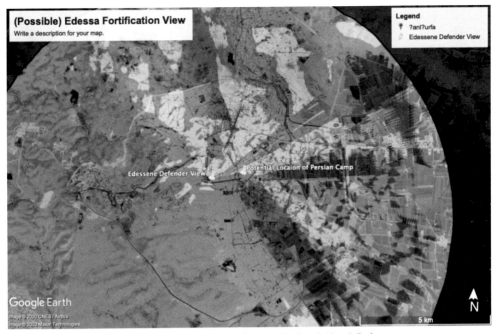

29. The possible fortification view from Edessa. (*Copyright Google Earth Pro*)

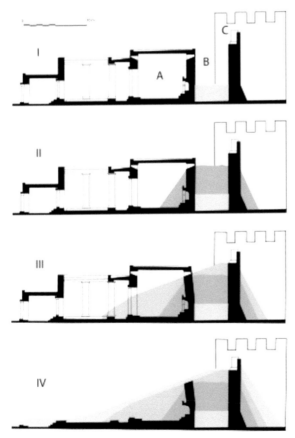

30. The siege mound at Dura Europos. (*Copyright Wikimedia Commons*)

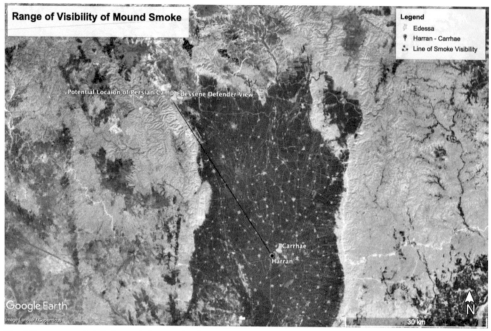

31. The range of visibility of the smoke from Edessa. (*Copyright Google Earth Pro*)

32. Abgar of Edessa receiving the Mandylion from Thaddeus, from Saint Catherine's Monastery, Egypt. (*Copyright Wikimedia Commons*)

Meanwhile in the city the victims of famine were dropping in their thousands, and there was suffering beyond description. In every house the mere flicker of a sight of food caused domestic warfare, and family members would fight each other to grab some pitiful means of keeping alive. Not even the dying could prove their destitution, but the terrorists would search bodies already at their last gasp, in case they were feigning death and had some food concealed in their clothing. Slack-jawed with hunger like mad dogs, the terrorists staggered about on their rounds, banging at doors like drunks, and in their far-gone state bursting into the same houses two or three times in a single hour. Necessity compelled people to put their teeth into anything they could find, and they would pick up and bring themselves to eat stuff which would not be fed even to the filthiest of animals. In the end they came down to gnawing belts and shoes, and stripping the leather off their shields to chew it. Some tried to sustain life on scraps of old hay, and there were people who collected the bare stalks and sold a minute bunch for four Attic drachmas.[8]

Thanks to recent research, we are well informed about the diet of first century CE inhabitants of Jerusalem.[9] In turn, some of this work sheds light on social hierarchies in the city. For instance, excavations have revealed that in the north, there is a relative abundance of pigeon remains, which is in stark contrast to what's been found in the city's southern landfill. Pigeons were used as sacrificial offerings for those lower down the city's pecking order, namely those who visited the temple in the city's north. With respect to diet, those in the north were more likely to consume those parts of animals, like sheep, goats, and to a lesser degree cattle, that were meat poor, while those from wealthier parts of the city were more likely to consume much richer cuts. In the course of a siege, as days turned into weeks, and weeks into months, the availability of meat would decrease, as it would for everything else, like the olives and lentils, the sorts of things locals might consume under ordinary circumstances. But desperate times call for desperate measures. Plus, though the members of different classes might eat differently in peacetime, a besieged city could be a great leveller of social inequality.

As dire as these circumstances seem, and the doglike behaviour coupled with the eating of shoes is dire indeed, Josephus moves from the general to the specific before he closes with the heartbreaking story of Mary.[10] The story of Mary stands out because of its unusual nature; though only one person, her experience helps bring to life the horror of siege warfare for civilians.[11] For Josephus, the story went like this:

There was a woman called Mary, daughter of Eleazar, who came from Transjordan, from the village of Bethezuba... Hers was a distinguished and wealthy family, and she had fled with the rest of that population to Jerusalem, where like everyone else she had to suffer the siege. The warlords had robbed her of most of the possessions she had packed up and brought with her to the city from Peraea, and what was left of her treasures, together with any food she managed to procure, was carried off in the daily invasions of their henchmen. The poor woman conceived a furious resentment, and her constant abuse of the looters and the curses she called down on them only provoked them further. When no one was exasperated or pitying enough to kill her, when she was exhausted by her efforts to find food which others would then take – and wherever she looked it was now impossible to find any food – and when hunger was coursing through every organ and bone in her body, and anger burning her up yet more fiercely than hunger, she allowed fury to join necessity in steering her to an act against all nature. She laid hands on her own child, an infant still at the breast. 'Poor baby,' she said to him, 'when all is war, famine, and party strife, should I keep you alive for any of these? With the Romans that means slavery, if we are still living when they come; but famine is faster on us than slavery, and the partisans are worse than either. So here we go: let's have you becoming food for me, an avenging ghost to haunt the partisans, and the one story the world still needs to complete the picture of Jewish suffering.' With that, she killed her son, roasted his body and ate half of it, then covered up and saved the rest. The partisans were there in no time, caught the smell of the unspeakable roast, and threatened her with instant execution unless she produced the dish she had prepared. Saying that she had kept a good portion for them, she brought out the remains of her child. The immediate effect was a horrified stupefaction, and they stood there frozen at the sight. She went on: 'This is my own lawful child, and this is my own doing. So eat! I have already eaten. Don't let yourselves be weaker than a woman or softer than a mother. But if you come over all pious and reject this sacrifice of mine, then let's say I have done your eating for you, and what's left should stay with me.' That sent them trembling on their way. This was the only case where their courage failed them, reluctant though they were to concede even this food to the mother. But the whole city was immediately filled with the news of this abomination, and everyone, picturing the tragic scene in their mind's eye, felt a shiver as if they themselves had gone that far. The starving longed for death, and thought the lucky ones were those who had met their end before they had word or sight of such horrors.[12]

As I said, this story illustrates well the human toll of siege warfare. Mary's actions, however, seem only to have soured Roman views of the Jews in the war, or so Josephus suggests. While not a combatant herself, the story illustrates well how siege warfare had a direct impact on all those involved, not just the soldiers. Mary's actions are horrifying and, as Josephus tells us, even if the residents of the city had reached their wits end, to kill, cook, and consume one's own child was too much. In other words, for the rest of the city, there was a limit to how far you should go during a famine. When push comes to shove, everyone has to eat, but not like this.

To get back to the bigger picture, the Romans attacked the Temple Mount, which they destroyed, a tactic possibly encouraged by Titus, though Josephus' trustworthiness on this is up for debate. In the course of the mayhem, the Romans looted the temple, taking all sorts of stuff. To make matters worse for the defeated, Roman standards were set up inside and sacrificed to, a sacrilegious act, and Titus was proclaimed '*imperator*', or conqueror.

Although the damage to the Temple Mount has arguably had the greatest impact over the longest period of time, there is good evidence for destruction on a smaller scale within individual structures. The Burnt House, for which only the basement survives, had the remains of a stone weight inscribed 'Bar Kathros'. Additionally, inside they found the remains of the arm of a young woman, in her 20s, who was trapped by the burning house and died.

We have no way of knowing more about the unfortunate victim. There are few starker examples of the impact of touch in war than this. The weight of the falling debris indubitably left its mark on her. Not knowing the whereabouts of the rest of her remains makes firm explanations elusive. Was the rest of her body given a proper burial elsewhere? After the collapse of some of the building's structure, in a mad push for survival, could she and/or a friend or family member have severed the arm from the rest of the body? But smell and taste, to some degree, factor too. The smell and taste of the smoke from the flames might have been unpleasant. She might have succumbed before things got this far. Finally, though we only know a little about her, her fate helps us to put a face on the human side of this conflict.

Those who weren't killed in acts of destruction like this, were likely rounded up and sold into slavery. Indeed, the scale of this was such that there was a drop in the prices because of glut. As Josephus notes,

> Now the number of those that were carried captive during this whole war was collected to be 97,000; as was the number of those that perished during the whole siege 1,100,000, the greater part of whom were indeed of the same nation [with the citizens of Jerusalem], but not belonging to the city itself; for they were come up from all the country to the feast of unleavened bread, and were on a sudden shut up by an army, which, at the very first, occasioned so great a straitness among them, that there came a pestilential destruction upon them, and soon afterward such a famine, as destroyed them more suddenly.[13]

Masada

Although the capture and destruction of Jerusalem effectively brought the war to an end, one site held out a little while longer, namely Masada (see Image 18). Famously, the defenders committed suicide to avoid capture by the Romans, at the end of a siege that lasted three to four years. More recent evidence, however, implies that this was not the case, with the siege possibly lasting six months if not a bit more, not a few years.[14]

Masada has been well excavated, and the site, like Jerusalem, has left us with a wealth of evidence about the experience of war. Archaeologists have identified and, in many cases, excavated a wide variety of different structures, from different gates and walls to assorted structures built during the reign of King Herod. Early during his tenure, the Parthians invaded and Herod, who had been based at Masada, travelled to Nabataea to ask for help, but to no avail. Thereafter, he went to Egypt, where Marc Antony agreed to step up. Then, in 40 BCE, he was given the title of King of Judea.

The kingdom expanded during the reign of Augustus, though there was considerable unrest, with various components of Herod's family opposed to his actions. Indeed, by some accounts he was tyrannical with his sons, and when he died he left the question of succession unresolved. More importantly for us, Herod undertook a major construction programme in Judea, with a lot of work carried out at Jerusalem and Caesarea. At Jerusalem, this included the construction of the palace. What's more, Herod renovated the Second Temple, built originally during the period of Persian occupation (sixth century BCE), and expanded the sacred precinct, which includes the now-famous wailing wall (originally part of the temenos, not the temple building itself).

Herod also carried out some significant work at Masada.[15] This included a pleasure-garden and large palace, which is still well-preserved. At the time of the war, the *sicarii*, a breakaway group of zealots, were the most likely group to occupy the site.[16] They weren't alone, however, for refugees came there from elsewhere, often in big family groups, and they camped wherever they could, often crowded into rooms. Those rooms that they occupied were often built into pre-existing structures.

There were plenty of facilities at Masada for the preparation and storage of food. Food was one of the most important components to a siege. We haven't discussed sieges in the previous chapters, so it's worth setting out the key stages here.[17] For one thing, manpower needs in a siege were high. To stem potential losses at the beginning, during the pre-contact stage, the attacking army might try to intimidate the defenders and force them to surrender. They might make direct pleas to the inhabitants. They might also make displays of strength by parading the army before the walls to frighten and intimidate those inside.

The attackers might employ additional means of intimidating those inside. They might flaunt their own supply of food to those on the inside, who, depending on what stage everything was unfolding, might get hungry themselves. If enemy leaders had been captured, they might be executed before the walls and in sight of the defenders. If they finally relented, they could find some solace in the fact that those who surrendered usually suffered better treatment than those whose towns were stormed.

Masada's location made the site easier to defend than most other locations, a detail which accounts, at least in part, for the amount of time it took the Romans to take the fortress.[18] Its elevated position made going under its fortifications difficult if not impossible. To compensate, the Romans constructed a massive siege ramp with a view to making it through or over the fortifications, at least at one spot.[19] Additionally, they built temporary camps, still visible, good evidence that they intended to be there for the long run. Indeed, these camps surrounded the city. The principal Roman camp, where the headquarters for the attackers was found, was full of luxury items (see Image 19). That camp even had stone platforms upon which commanders might speak, and *triclinia*, Roman couches, which were orientated towards Masada, so offering those in charge a clear view of the town while they were dining.[20]

Circumvallation, surrounding a location with a wall, palisade or earthwork was one of the primary things a besieging army might try, at least where possible. Some places were too big, but others weren't. The attackers might try to set up a blockade, to prevent supplies from getting to the defenders. If the decision was made to force an entry into the locale, there were three ways to get into a defended (ie walled) site: you could go under the walls, you could go over the walls, or you could go through them. The attackers might employ surprise, tricks and treachery.

An attacking Roman army might employ any number of artillery machines to get through the walls, like onagers, *ballistae*, and catapults.[21] Assorted missiles from artillery have been found throughout the site, and it seems that bolts were collected and recycled.[22] A significant part of the sensory experience of any siege would be the sight of the missiles flying through the air towards the walls, as well as the sound of those missiles, both while moving through the air and then when they crashed into the walls. Soldiers might also employ battering rams to bust down doors or gates to get into a fortified town or city. For those in the immediate vicinity, the sound of the machine crashing against the doors would have been distinctive. As it happens, many of these were applied at Masada. Rams were brought up repeatedly to the city's wall that managed to effect a breach, only for the Romans to discover what was going on inside. Yet another means of besting a site's walls was by creating holes in the walls, inserting wood chips, and then setting them alight with a view to bringing the walls down. Mines too were another option, but I'll return to those in Chapter 6.

Their determination to get in was motivated by a number of things, like booty, rape, alcohol, the hatred of the enemy, and to attain honour. Speed too was critical: the quicker an attacking army could take the city, the less the logistical challenges a prolonged siege would present. Indeed, the Romans would offer incentives to attackers, with awards given to the first man over the walls. Josephus describes a speech made by Titus in his *Jewish War* in which the Flavian general does his best to motivate his men to scale the walls at Jerusalem.[23]

The defenders, on the other hand, would have their fortifications as the main obstacle, and would employ a range of tools to fight off the attackers, like javelins, arrows, and even rocks, boiling water, and burning oil. If possible, they would use artillery and assorted machinery. Sorties, where groups of soldiers charged out from the defences against the attackers, might also be employed. Critical, however, was to maintain clear communications – and even more so, adequate supplies, primarily of things to eat and drink.

Ultimately, Masada proved to be a significant logistical challenge both for the Romans and more recently when the site was rediscovered, and excavations began. Today, you can access the site by means of a difficult hike or a cable car. Eventually, the Romans constructed a massive siege ramp (see Image 20), visible to this day, which allowed them to overcome the site's artificial fortifications as well as the natural ones. At some point after it was completed, they began the assault.[24]

As noted, however, the siege took quite a long time, even if what Josephus records doesn't match what the archaeological evidence tells us. Although the Romans could be ruthless and mechanistic – and Josephus' digression on their training is a big reason why many have referred to the Roman military as a machine – they could also be patient. It seems likely that the Romans spent a lot of time waiting out the *sicarii* and others at Masada, with a view to lessening their resolve. Indeed, both the literary evidence provided by Josephus and the material evidence that has come from the multiple excavations has revealed a great deal about the hunger that afflicted the defenders. Indeed, there's nothing like a siege to reveal the potential disparity in diets of the opposing sides – and its ability to equalize the diet of those who are besieged, a point stressed by Smith.

In the case of Masada, its location made ready access of food and water difficult to achieve.[25] Indeed, near the start of this stage of the siege, Josephus says, 'though in other respects it presented difficulties for the maintenance of supplies. Not only had food to be brought in from a distance, involving very exhausting work for the Jews put on this detail, but drinking water too had to be imported, as there was no spring in the immediate neighbourhood'.[26] On the other hand, as far as the defenders are concerned:

> The plateau itself had rich soil softer than any lowland plain, and King Herod gave it up to cultivation, so that if ever the supply of food from outside was cut off, that would not have serious impact on those who had trusted the fortress to keep them safe.[27]

Additionally, regarding Herod's building programme at Masada:

> At every place where people lived, on the summit, round the palace, fronting the walls, he had excavated in the rock many large tanks as reservoirs, to create a water supply as good as that enjoyed where there is access to springs.[28]

Indeed, Masada had been so well provisioned that, when Eleazar, the rebel leader, took the site, he found the following:

> But yet more remarkable was the spectacular store of provisions laid up inside – and their state of preservation. Stored here was a mass of corn, amply enough to last for years, and an abundance of wine and oil, as well as pulses of every sort and piles of dates. When Eleazar and his sicarii took the fortress by surprise, they found all these stores still fresh and just as good as new produce laid in. And yet it was nearly a century from the original provisioning of the fortress to its capture by the Romans, and the Romans also found what remained of the food stores undecayed.[29]

Josephus' comments here are all well and good – and he is clearly aware of the role of food and supplies in warfare, particularly sieges – but he seems to have been misled, or he outright fabricated significant aspects of his siege narrative. For as it happens, excavations have revealed a good deal about the kinds of food found at Masada and consumed by those besieged, and it doesn't quite match up with what we find in the *Jewish War*.

From what we know, the refugee families discussed earlier crowded into rooms, which were built into existing structures, and these structures were well equipped for the preparation and storage of food. The rooms were well-stocked with food and water, and archaeologists have found jars filled with all sorts of goods.[30] Though the contents are for the most part long gone, there is enough of what remains to tell us what was inside. Inscriptions labelled the goods in the jars, and seeds have allowed us to learn more about what sorts of things they kept in storage. This meant things like dried figs, berries, olives, fish, dough, meat, and herbs. On this account, then, the evidence would seem, to some degree or other, to support what Josephus said.

Josephus claimed that the food had remained at Masada from its expansion under Herod to the *sicarii* occupation, and then the Roman one, and in relatively good shape at that. In this case, the evidence on the ground tells a different story, and reveals a great deal about the suffering of the besieged. Based on the evidence found on site, the conditions were harsh. The diet of the ordinary consisted of bread dipped in olive oil, bean pastes like hummus, and lentil stews. While to me that all sounds well and delicious, the excavations revealed that their food was infested with pests.[31] The kind of damage these pests would have caused and the variety of insects found is remarkable. Some were well suited to life in the storage bins where the grain was stored.[32] There are also insects that savage those very grain-infesting insects.[33] As for the identification of the pests found at Masada, they include the sawtoothed grain beetle, the lesser grain borer, the wheat weevil, the date store beetle, the flat grain beetle, and many more besides.[34] Indeed, it seems a significant proportion of their food supply was infested with pests, bugs, with remains of both the insects themselves and their larvae recovered. So while they might have had food to eat at the end, it wasn't in great shape. In this siege, like many others, ordinary tasks like eating and drinking – taste and smell – were severely impacted by the ongoing conflict.

Before I close the chapter, it's worth saying a few things about who in particular suffered at Masada – who were the ones eating that spoiled food? Josephus' story implies that it was a large group of rebels. The material finds from the site reveal that the population was far more varied, as I've already indicated. It seems there were a lot of women and children at Masada, as Josephus implies, but which the archaeological finds confirm. Amongst the many personal artefacts found which are often (but not always) associated with women, were jewellery and cosmetic items.[35] This included palette, eye shadow sticks, bottles for perfume, and combs. Not only did this material confirm the varied backgrounds of the inhabitants of Masada near its end, but it also revealed more about their conditions, for there were hints of lice and their eggs in amongst this evidence. Despite all this, it seems the synagogue on site continued in use, with the observation of Jewish rituals continuing during the siege.

Ultimately, the siege came to an end. According to Josephus, it ended something like this:

> They then chose ten men by lot, out of them; to slay all the rest. Every one of whom laid himself down by his wife, and children, on the ground, and threw his arms about them, and they offered their necks to the stroke of those who by lot executed that melancholy office. And when these ten had, without fear, slain them all, they made the same rule for casting lots for themselves; that he whose lot it was should first kill the other nine; and after all should kill himself. Accordingly all these had courage sufficient to be no way behind one another in doing or suffering. So, for a conclusion, the nine offered their necks to the executioner; and he who was the last of all took a view of all the other bodies; lest perchance some or other among so many that were slain should want his assistance to be quite dispatched: and when he perceived that they were all slain, he set fire to the palace, and with the great force of his hand ran his sword entirely through himself, and fell down dead near to his own relations. So these people died with this intention, that they would not leave so much as one soul among them all alive to be subject to the Romans. Yet was there an ancient woman, and another who was of kin to Eleazar, and superior to most women in prudence and learning, with five children, who had concealed themselves in caverns underground; and had carried water thither for their drink; and were hidden there when the rest were intent upon the slaughter of one another. Those others were nine hundred and sixty in number: the women, and children being withal included in that computation. This calamitous slaughter was made on the fifteenth day of the month Xanthicus [Nisan].[36]

Though this image has been part of the legend of Masada for quite some time, the reality is that the excavations revealed no evidence of a mass suicide – that is, there was no major collection of human remains.

While this shouldn't downgrade their suffering, it does mean that their ultimate fate remains an open question.

The varied evidence from Masada, the archaeological evidence in particular, gives us remarkable insight into the sensory experience at Masada. All those inside, besieged by Romans, would have to taste and smell all sorts of unpleasant things, especially connected to their food supply. Much of the food was in rough shape and despite the unsightly appearance of pests in the food, they'd also have to deal with the odour from food gone off.

Bar Kokhba

This book is focused squarely on the sensory experience of pitched battles and sieges, with the odd exception. At the end of this chapter, I want to draw attention to another of these exceptions, something that could be called a siege, but is probably best categorized as an 'other' form of combat – or just an instance of violence, carried out by Roman soldiers, at the end of yet another brutal war. To stay consistent with the material of this chapter, I'm going to finish by jumping ahead to the war that followed several decades later, what is usually called the Bar Kokhba Revolt. Although many of the circumstances were different, there is one particularly detailed story attached to this war that allows us to look a little deeper into the sensory experiences of non-combatants in armed conflict with imperial Rome. Plus, though this episode comes much later, it's easy to imagine similar groups of rebels pursued by Roman soldiers in analogous scenarios during the earlier, much more famous, war.

The story centres on the Babatha archive, the personal documents of a woman named Babatha, who might well have been illiterate, but who had a scribe. Judging by what we find in her papers, her personal documents written down on some papyrus scrolls, she seems to have been married twice, and to have had one son by her first husband. Babatha was Jewish, but she lived in Nabataea not long after the kingdom was annexed by the Romans, under Trajan, in the early second century CE. She lived in the village of Maoza on the southeast coast of the Dead Sea.

So far as we know, it all came to an end for her when she fled en-Gedi during the Bar Kokhba Revolt with rebel sympathizers and hid in a cave, which came to be known as The Cave of Letters (Image 21). This cave served as a hideout, but the Romans knew they were there. One of the things the Roman approach reveals is their ruthless and calculated approach to insurgencies, at least in this instance.[37] They built a temporary fort or camp below with a view to waiting them out, at least for a time. Eventually, however, their patience wore thin and they stormed the cave. Though we don't know the ultimate fate of Babatha and her companions, it seems pretty clear at least she (if not they, too) didn't make it back. They might have been executed somewhere else, or in her case or those of any other women and children there, they might have been sold off into slavery. Some skulls, wrapped in textiles, were found in the cave and might date to this episode, but we don't know specifics.

We don't know what the conditions were for her in the cave, though it's easy to imagine them running out of things to eat and drink before too long – and in far less time than it took those at Masada decades earlier. Babatha took care to hide some of her prized possessions, however, which were tucked away in a spot inside the cave that she had likely intended to return to in the future. Amongst this remarkable collection of materials was a number of papyri all belonging to her, which provide a legal history of some property she owned on or near the Dead Sea. The earliest one dates to 94 CE, the latest to the years shortly before the Bar Kokhba revolt. These papyri were written in Aramaic, Greek, Hebrew, and Nabataean, and these reveal all sorts of interesting and valuable details about life in this corner of the world in the early second century CE. We learn, for instance, that the Nabataeans had a fully-formed culture with their own towns, language, scribes, laws, gods, and more. They show too that relations between the Nabataeans and Jews were pretty good, despite some serious conflicts between the two neighbouring kingdoms in the first century CE. These papyri also inform us about the transition, in the region, from independent kingdom (Nabataea, centred on Petra) to Roman province (Arabia).[38]

One of the most remarkable things about this collection of papyri (and the few other assorted finds from the cave) is the insight it gives us into one woman's life, a figure from a group (women) which doesn't often have much of a voice in more traditional evidence, like narrative histories. For instance, thanks to these papyri, we know that she was illiterate, but that she could afford a scribe to do the work for her, not unlike many others, both men and women. We learn that she had been married twice, with one son by her first husband. We know too that she was a Jewish woman living in Nabataea a couple of decades after the place had been annexed by Rome. As far as the subject of this book is concerned, all of this helps us put a face to the lived experience of this one civilian in an ancient conflict.[39]

To get back to the sensory experience of this conflict, we can well imagine that life in the cave, however long it was, would have been challenging, and Babatha was probably filled with fear throughout this ordeal. Assuming she had the full use of all of her senses, there were likely severe limitations on what she could eat and drink inside what was probably a dull, and often dark, cave. On the other hand, the cause of her consternation, the Roman soldiers, would never have been far from view. If she looked out the cave's entrance, she could probably see them below. At night, she'd be able to see the flames, and maybe even smell the smoke, from their fires. Being cramped, possibly for days, if not more, inside a cave meant she could probably feel the evening chill and, more often than not, her companions. She probably kept her son, however old he might have been when all this happened, close, possibly during the day and almost certainly at night. For Babatha, and others like her, this war was an assault on her senses, and assuming she made it out alive, it would have been a sensory experience unlike any she is likely to have gone through before.

In looking at these three sieges from two related conflicts in Judea, we get a good sense of the sensory experience of those who arguably suffered the most, the civilians. The invaluable evidence also presents us with useful information on those we often know less about, the women and children. Although warfare in the ancient Mediterranean was often fought by men, its impact was far reaching.

Part III

Late Antiquity

Chapter 5

The Battle of Strasbourg (357 CE)

The Roman Empire changed considerably from the third
century into the fourth, with the very capital itself replaced, at
least politically, by places like Trier (see Image 22). These new
imperial capitals often boasted of thicker and higher walls, a reflection
of the increased militarization of the Empire. One of the most famous
emperors from late antiquity also had one of the shortest reigns,
namely Julian, who ruled from 361 to 363 CE. Indeed, one of the most
famous battles of late antiquity is the Battle of Strasbourg, in which
the Romans under their Caesar Julian defeated an Alamanni army in
357 CE. While the battle has not received the same level of attention
as other ancient battles like Marathon and Cannae, its chief historian,
Ammianus Marcellinus, and its leading commander Julian, have not
been left wanting.[1] In this chapter, I explore how a sensory approach to
the battle at Strasbourg, which includes the five most familiar senses
(sight, sound, touch, smell, and taste), can reveal a great deal about the
lived experiences of the participants on the field of battle, both the elite
and the common soldiery. I argue that using the senses provides a solid
framework for understanding some disparate parts of the battle as well
as the account provided by our chief source, Ammianus Marcellinus.

Ammianus and Strasbourg

The Roman world of Strasbourg was not the same world we met at
Masada. In the intervening three centuries, the Roman army had
grown, but so too had its problems. There were still plenty of legions
and auxiliary units, only they were smaller, and likely wouldn't look
quite the same as their earlier versions. There were also plenty of new
unit types. The role of cavalry too had continued to grow in the Roman
military, and we see this at Strasbourg.[2]

The fourth century world was much more bureaucratic too, with more provinces and more officials, and even more emperors, depending on the year. Julian, who would become emperor in 361 (361–363 CE), was then, in 359, a Caesar under his uncle Constantius II (r. 337–361 CE), one of the sons – and the most successful – of Constantine I (r. 306–337 CE). These late antique emperors were autocratic, but in the fourth century they still worked hard to appear regularly before their citizens, wherever they were. In fact, this was rarely Rome, which was no longer the city it had been, even if it was still home to the Senate, whereas Constantinople was not yet the city it would later become.

As noted, the principal source for this battle and era was the last great Latin Roman historian, Ammianus Marcellinus. Ammianus was a well-heeled Greek who wrote, in Latin, a multi-volume history of Rome until about 378 CE, or shortly after the disastrous of Battle of Adrianople. Only a portion of his *Res Gestae* survives, and it covers about twenty-five years, from 353 to 378, with the original starting from the reign of Nerva. It's highly detailed and covers most of the kinds of subjects that histories of its type had been covering for centuries: war, politics, and whatever else caught one's eye.[3] Much of the *Res Gestae* is filled with war and warfare, and scholars have shown some interest in his treatment of these topics, particularly his crafting of battle narratives. Many now accept that Ammianus showed considerable interest in the experience of soldiers in battle in his accounts, though questions have been raised about whether his artfulness has obfuscated his writing.[4]

Ammianus doesn't just describe the battle at Strasbourg with the Alamanni. He also provides much of the background too. His account of the battle comes in the last chapter of book sixteen of his thirty-one-book *Res Gestae*, with the previous chapters of that same book providing the background (and other things). The book is largely concerned with Rome's war with the Alamanni, with the Romans under Julian pulling off a series of victories. Julian attacked the Alamanni, slaughtering, capturing, and ultimately vanquishing them – or so Ammianus.[5] The general Julian then moved to capture Cologne, where he made an agreement with a Frank king and took the city.[6] Not long after, Julian advanced to the town of Sens, where he was besieged by the Alamanni.[7] He survived, and afterwards launched an attack on the Alamanni on the islands on the Rhine, whence they had fled. Julian also reinforced Tres Tabernae, which brings us up to Strasbourg.[8] The conflict in the build-up to Strasbourg wasn't the first time the two parties had come up against each other. The first encounters came over a century earlier, and though the Alamanni are, from a Roman perspective, usually characterized as a worthy enemy, some have argued that they were a manufactured enemy, a people an emperor or leading general could engage in combat with a view to a secure and reputable victory.[9] It's possible to get a sense of this here at Strasbourg in Ammianus' telling, for the size of the two armies has probably been exaggerated; as is, Julian's army is modest. Nevertheless, his description makes for a great story.

The Battle of Strasbourg pitted Julian and his mixed army of Roman soldiers against a much larger Alamannic force. The distance from the Roman camp to the Alamnnic one was about 33 kilometres.[10] As the Roman army advanced, they approached a hill with a gentle slope covered with grain and not far from the Rhine.[11] The Alamanni had been crossing the river for three days and three nights in the build-up. One of the most detailed parts of Ammianus' description of the battle is his catalogue of forces, particularly on the Roman side, though also the Alamanni. Catalogues of forces like this were a staple of many descriptions of combat, with all extant ones ultimately going back to the war at Troy and Homer's *Iliad*, book two of which contained a long and detailed catalogue of the Greek and Trojan forces. At this battle, a millennium to a millennium-and-a-half later, on the Roman side, the leading figure was Julian, then a Caesar (not yet emperor).[12] Other key figures included the praetorian prefect Florentius and Severus, another general at the battle.[13] Although he may not identify them all precisely, he does tell us a bit about the different kinds of soldiers fighting on the Roman side. Some of it is generic, like Julian's followers and some brave men. But he also identifies some infantry forces, squadrons of cavalry, and cataphracts, as well as soldiers in companies.[14] Ammianus also identifies Cornuti and Bracchiati and the soldiers of one particular legion (Primani).[15] On the Alamanni side, there were seven kings, Chonodomarius, Vestralpus, Urius, Ursicinus, Serapio, Suomarius, and Hortarius.[16] They also had a number of princes and nobles. Ammianus is a little less particular about the character of their army.

Ammianus' Appeals to the Senses

Ammianus Marcellinus' writing is some of the most vivid from the ancient world, and while this means that a good chunk of the narrative was likely embellished for rhetorical effect, it still manages to capture much of the sensory appeal of combat. Before I turn to some specific examples, there are some more generic ones that help to enliven the action.

Ammianus describes the beams of the sun reddening the sky on the fateful day, clouds of dust, with standards prominently displayed.[17] Some of those are the dragon standard, which Ammianus describes in detail:

> On recognising him by the purple ensign of a dragon, fitted to the top of a very long lance and spreading out like the slough of a serpent, the tribune of one of the squadrons stopped, and pale and struck with fear rode back to renew the battle.[18]

Besides the sights, there are also the sounds, the gnashing and grinding of teeth, and the striking of spears and shields together.[19] There's shouting, and trumpeters, calling soldiers to battle.[20] Altogether, the sky echoes with cries.

Ammianus' language is poetic, rhetorical, and shares features with some other fourth century accounts of battle, like the panegyrists who sang the praises of the empire's soldiers. Some scholars have characterized Ammianus' approach as a 'face of battle' style, referring to the famous book by John Keegan.[21] Keegan argued that the balance should shift from commanders to the ordinary soldiers who play such a big role in combat. So, Keegan examined the experiences of soldiers in battle. The argument of these other scholars, then, is that Ammianus did this too. Ross goes further and sees this as a distinctive feature of much battle narrative in late antiquity.[22] This tendency can be tied, at least in part, to the shared background and training of authors like this, historians and panegyrists, in the fourth century (and much of Roman history for that matter). Rhetorical handbooks, sometimes called *progymnasmata*, made up a big part of their training, and these works were filled with instructions about what sorts of things authors should be composing. This included detailed descriptions, *ekphrases*, which were meant to bring the thing being described before the eyes of the reader – or the listener if a composition was presented orally. One way to pull this off was to appeal to the reader's or the listener's senses. Indeed, by most ancient definitions of *ekphrases*, this was what they were meant to do.[23] Before we get back to battle, a word on its connection with *ekphrases*. For ancient rhetoricians, and the historians influenced by their writings, a battle was a description, an *ekphrasis*, that would have these features. In other words, battles and senses go hand-in-hand. Let's now get back to Strasbourg.

One of the hallmarks of ancient set-piece battles is the pre-battle exhortation. Most ancient historians make them out to be long-winded affairs, an issue I touched on in the first chapter while looking at Xenophon. They surface, too, in the chapters on Cannae and Masada/ Jerusalem. In works of ancient history, not only do they tend to be long-winded, but they are often (but not always) matched by an attendant speech by the opposite side, which responds to the points raised in the first speech. Given the order in which they're presented in most texts, this is plainly impossible, especially if the different participants don't speak the same language. But speeches were given before battle in some form or other, and what stands out about Ammianus in this battle is that most of his accounts of speeches are believable. The exception is the first one.

Ammianus highlights the words and sound of Julian's speech by contrasting the actions of his soldiers beforehand. He describes the silence and calmness in anticipation of what he is about to say.[24] When the time comes, the speech that Julian gives near the start of the battle is full of some important points to remember. He stresses that he and his soldiers are fellow soldiers and while he notes their courage he urges them to be cautious and circumspect. The soldiers were angry and exhausted by the marching, for the weather had been hot and water had been hard to come by.[25] So, rather than rushing off to battle against the Alamanni while weary from travel, they should wait until they've had a chance to recover and they get a suitable signal from God. Ammianus presents this speech as a dialogue, however, for we get a reply from an unnamed standard bearer, who says he's a brave general with good counsel, while also warlike and with the favour of the supreme deity.[26] This is enough to push Julian to engage their foes. But we should note too that several senses feature prominently in his speech.

A bit later Ammianus makes it clear that a full speech before the troops was impossible for a number of reasons, namely, 'on account of the wide extent of the field and the great numbers of the multitude that had been brought together'.[27] Thus, instead he gives a number of similar speeches as he moves amongst the ranks on horseback. He refers to similar little speeches in some other places in the text, and Ammianus implies that he regularly rode amongst the men and did this.[28] These are the most realistic portrayals of speeches that Ammianus or most other ancient historians give. For Ammianus Marcellinus, communications involving a commander like Julian were best effected by him personally moving amongst the men and speaking himself.

Sound

Ammianus' vivid account gives a good sense of the difficulty in hearing anything clearly. There was shouting from both sides, and, as he describes it, the loud cries echoed in the skies. Some of those cries, at least near the beginning, would have been the war cries found in most if not all pre-modern battles. The war cry we find at Strasbourg was the *barritus*, given by select Roman soldiers, called Carnuti, to intimidate others. Most of its particulars are unclear, though Ammianus does gives us some clues, even here: '[it] rises from a low murmur and gradually grows louder, like waves dashing against the cliffs'.[29] This isn't the only spot that Ammianus discusses the *barritus*. When Constantius speaks to his Roman troops (21.13.15), '*barritus*' means a generic war cry. Several books later, the term appears in the midst of a speech given by the usurper Procopius to two would-be opposing armies. In this speech, Procopius says the *barritus* comes in his description of the Battle of Adrianople. In this case, he gives some idea of how it might have worked: 'as usual rising from a low to a louder tone, of which the national name is *barritus*, and thus roused themselves to mighty strength'.[30] In that battle, the barbarians gave shouts of their own: songs that praised the glories of their forefathers mixed with wild, discordant, shouts. While the Goths of Adrianople weren't the Alamanni of Strasbourg, there's no reason to suspect that they wouldn't be singing comparable songs of their own.

The most we can glean about the character of the *barritus* is that it goes from a lower to a louder tone. Tacitus describes what might be the *barritus'* precursor in a little more depth in the *Germania*. For him, 'it's not…an articulate sound…They aim chiefly at a harsh note and a confused roar, putting their shields to their mouth, so that, by reverberation, it may swell into a fuller and deeper sound'.[31] What that might have sounded like in practice is hard to say. In the funerary scene for Marcus Aurelius from the 1964 film *The Fall of Rome*, the soldiers give some sort of murmur that's not unlike what Tacitus and Ammianus describe, though the setting is entirely different. There it's a moody, even haunting, cry. Is this what we might have expected at Strasbourg? Hard to say, though the notes in the movie don't strike me as particularly low, which is in contrast to what Ammianus says. I wonder too if there might not have been some distinct words used as part of the cry. Nevertheless, we have every reason to suppose that whatever sound it might have been, it would have had an impact on those both making and hearing the sound, much as that scene does in the film.

The *barritus* wasn't the only part of the soundscape of Strasbourg, however, for Roman trumpets played a big part in the battle, and for good reason. At several points in the battle narrative, Ammianus alludes to the role of trumpets. At 16.12.7, in its early stages, Ammianus tells us that the trumpets sounded, which served to commence the march from the Roman camp to the Alamanni one. The next reference to the sounding of the trumpets comes at 16.12.27, where the trumpets blared ominously. At 16.12.36, the trumpets called men to battle; and lastly, at 16.12.45, the trumpets played a savage note.

Musical instruments played a role in communicating a host of things in Roman battles. By some accounts, the horn was used to indicate the start of battle, while the trumpet was used to indicate different manoeuvres. In the earliest surviving book of the *Res Gestae* in a speech given by Emperor Constantius II, Ammianus implies that the very noise of the trumpet was associated with combat.[32] Indeed, a bit later Ammianus refers to a trumpet (*tuba*) in the context of treason trials and feels the need to specify that it is a 'trumpet of court trials', (*iudicialium tuba in crimen*), which implies that a trumpet, when referred to with any sort of qualifier, is a wartime instrument.[33] In fact, the 'trumpet of court trials' is but one of several such cases where Ammianus uses instruments in a metaphorical sense, or so it's been argued.[34] Interestingly enough, the word he uses here is *tuba*, which by most definitions is a generic trumpet. On occasion he uses the more accurate *classicum*, which is usually defined specifically as a war trumpet. The sense, however, is that even the basic trumpet, *tuba*, is in Ammianus' eyes an instrument of war.[35]

Although we have been talking about the use of trumpets at Strasbourg, this was not the only potential instrument that participants might have heard in the course of the battle, nor is it the only instrument referred to by Ammianus.[36] Ammianus refers to the *lituus*, a slightly curved war trumpet used a lot like the *tuba*. In one instance it sounds the retreat,[37] and in another it starts the battle.[38] Ammianus also refers to the *bucina*, a curved war trumpet, though possibly a bugle too, on a few occasions.[39] It's used to wake the soldiers in the morning, and to signal assorted manoeuvres on the field of battle.[40] Ammianus also refers to *tubicines*, *cornicines*, *liticines*, and *aeneatores*.[41] As it happens, there are all sorts of instruments connected to the army; there's scattered evidence for additional instruments and musicians travelling along with soldiers on campaigns and even accompanying them in far off places.[42]

Sight

From sound we move to sight, and as much as Ammianus' vivid description serves to enliven the story and entertain his audience, the imagery does provide insight into other aspects of this battle and others: the trauma of combat. The graphic description of battle wounds had excellent literary pedigree, with Homer infusing his *Iliad* with all sorts of gruesome wounds and dramatic deaths. Ammianus doesn't include the kind of episodes that Procopius later does, nor as did the now-lost historians from a couple of centuries earlier, whom Lucian lambasts. Ammianus' account does, however, detail the experience of combat, and he includes information on the wounds, weapons, and suffering of both sets of soldiers. Indeed, according to Ammianus, you could see a number of things on the battlefield: in the midst of the combat you could see blade striking against blade, and swords crashing against breastplates;[43] when the battle turned the Romans started slashing the backs of the barbarians.[44] The Alamanni fought on determinedly, even while wounded and with their blood shed.[45] Many lay pierced with mortal wounds; some looked around for one last time; others had heads severed by pikes heavy as beams, with heads hanging down; some had fallen on the slippery ground; and others, still, were crushed by the weight of those falling on top of them.[46]

Not only has there been some fairly recent research on the psychological impact of battle, but also on the impact of ancient weapons and the types of wounds that soldiers might have received. Our physical evidence for battle wounds from antiquity is sparse. Only a limited number of skeletons from men who died in battle have been recovered; more often than not, the dead were cremated. Additionally, many of the potential wounds, regardless of their impact, would have involved damage to soft tissue alone, and so they wouldn't appear in the record, such as it is. That said, using comparative data from other pre-modern eras in combination with the abundant material from contemporary trauma centres has been illuminating, at least with respect to the range of potential injuries, their physiological effect, and the result on the combatants. Using this information in combination with the details in Ammianus' account, the kinds of injuries that we find include an assortment of possible penetrating injuries to the head, throat and neck, torso, and limbs; and blunt injuries to those same parts of the body. Of course, different injuries would affect soldiers in different ways. Serious injury to the head or torso could easily result in loss of life, while bruises to limbs or dust in the eyes, though possibly painful, were less likely to result in death, at least directly. Ammianus clearly only skims the surface, but those that he does mention cover all three of the major, potential, outcomes to battlefield wounds: rapidly fatal, incapacitating, and decreased mobility. During the battle, one group of Alamanni soldiers,[47] those with penetrating wounds, didn't have much time left; another group, who had been slashed in the back, were certainly incapacitated if not worse;[48] while yet another group, those who had slipped, might only have suffered decreased mobility.[49] In just a few lines, then, Ammianus described the full array of potential wound-types seen in the battle, even if his emphasis was primarily on penetrating injuries – javelins sunk into vitals and the like.

Touch

The sights and sounds of battle were only one side of the coin, for Ammianus also spends a surprising amount of time on the tactile experience of battle, especially the physical toil that long, intense, combat could have on its participants. This fourth-century battle involved not just the parrying and sword play that we often associate with ancient combat, but a physical shove of the sort we usually associate with the warfare of Greek city states. At 16.12.37, he describes the pressure the Alamanni applied through their knees – I'm sure we are to understand the full force of their legs – in an attempt to push back the Roman soldiers. This pushing intensifies, as shield-boss pushed against shield.[50] Indeed, in Ammianus' telling, the close order of the Roman troops played a major role in their victory. Several times, Ammianus describes their formations in terms of strong, compact, physical bodies. So, we hear about the Roman officers forming their men into a solid line, which was like an impregnable wall, to counter the Alamannic wedge formation.[51] These aren't simply examples of Ammianus stylizing his account, for there's good reason to think that fourth-century Romans did use pseudo-phalanx formations in combat, when needed.[52] Depending on the context and the source, the space between lines and soldiers in battle might range between 45 and 90cm, which is close enough to feel the body heat of one's neighbour. To make an effective *testudo*, however, you might need to stand closer still, and when the fighting was fiercest the Romans did just that.[53] In these cases, not only were you likely to feel your comrades beside you, unless you were on the ends, but also, quite possibly, in front and behind you too. As the handful of surviving ancient depictions indicate, an effective, tight, *testudo* would look very much like an impregnable wall (see Image 23).

A consideration of the differing tactics of the two sides reveal another facet of the tactile experience. The Romans deployed a significant number of heavy cavalry soldiers in the battle, and the sight of these cataphracts led to a reshuffle on the part of the Alamanni. It also revealed some of the limitations of their own cavalry, for the Alamanni had trouble holding onto all those things they would need to counter the Romans: their reins, shields, and spears.[54] There are other cases, later in the battle, where the holding of weapons became difficult, which in turn highlights the intensity of the fighting. At times the Romans' swords bent while attacking the Alamanni, a clear sign of overuse. In response, the Romans would seize Alamannic weaponry and use those instead.[55] Even if the swords didn't bend, so making them inoperable, the near constant swordplay led to their dulling as the battle raged.[56] To make matters worse, at least for the Alamanni, as the battle started to turn heavily in the Romans' favour, they had to deal not only with avoiding the helmets and shields rolling around the ground and the physical obstacle of a pile of bodies, but also with the real prospect of coming to further harm because of those same impediments. To make matters worse, in dodging bodies and equipment, the Alamanni, and Romans for that matter, also had to deal with the slippery ground, drenched in blood. If they did trip over the debris strewn across the field, there was the very real prospect that they might get crushed by the bodies of their comrades falling on top of them, as Ammianus points out.[57]

As we saw earlier, there were a range of wound types on the field of battle, and these ranged between the breaking of bones and head wounds, to wounds to the chest and abdomen. Not only were these injuries visible on the field of battle, but they were also felt by those so wounded. There are a few places where Ammianus conveys something of the pain felt by the combatants – those wounded, dead and dying. For instance, some of the Alamanni looked into the light with dying eyes,[58] so hinting at their pain, while others, in Ammianus' words, 'pierced with mortal wounds', begged for death.[59] Ammianus also refers to the groans of the dying, admittedly an audible thing, but it alludes to the pain felt by some soldiers.[60] Besides the pain there was also the exhaustion. Yet again, Ammianus draws attention to the Alamanni. He notes, for example, that the legs of some gave out, but they fought on, even if on one knee.[61] Thus, not only was there a lot to see and hear at Strasbourg, but a lot to feel.

Taste/Smell

To this point, I haven't touched on smell and taste of battle, which, admittedly, are less outwardly apparent in what evidence we have for ancient battles. To do this, however, we need to contemplate something the Romans could see during the battle rather than smell or taste. In the midst of combat, Ammianus paused to comment how 'the Alamanni were stronger and taller' than the Romans.[62] While this phrase is certainly a broad generalization, which reflects some level of bias on Ammianus' part, does it also conceal some kernel of truth? It could, for instance, be a case of Ammianus nodding to the historiographical, or pseudo-historiographical, tradition, for Caesar comments on the shorter stature of the Romans in comparison to the Gauls during his account of the campaigns against the Belgae.[63]

On the other hand, over the past decade or two, students of the Roman and late antique worlds have made increasing use of scientific evidence. One area of relevance to us is the health and wellbeing of ancient people, and a means of measuring this is by analysing ancient skeletons.[64] Following from this, there have been several attempts to measure the stature of ancient Mediterranean populations and beyond, an exercise which has had mixed – and contentious – results.[65] To determine height, perhaps rather obviously, scholars have had to measure the length of the skeletons from cemeteries in Italy and assorted sites in Europe. Although debate has raged over whether one of the most commonly used measures for height in antiquity, the length of the femur, is as reliable as it might, on the surface, seem, some sort of consensus has been reached. Most would argue that during the imperial era, a high point in terms of material wellbeing in Roman history, the average Roman was on the short side.[66] There has also been some comparable work on early medieval populations in northern and central Europe, the lands from which the Alamanni hailed; they seem to have been taller than their Roman neighbours.[67] In fact, in many such regions their height seems to have peaked in the fifth and sixth centuries CE, not long after Ammianus was writing his account.

The point of looking more closely at Ammianus' comment about height wasn't solely to test his veracity, but to explore the role of taste and smell in battle. Another side of the scientific approach to the ancient world is the connection between height and diet. The residents of northern and central Europe, even when significant chunks of their territory fell under Roman rule, seem to have consumed much more cattle and dairy products than their southern neighbours.[68] In southern Europe – closer to the Mediterranean – when it came to meat, pork was preferred. And in the east, it was goats and sheep. Depending on where the soldiers were from, then, we might well expect to smell a range of meats, if not just before battle in their camps, at least back in their forts.

Although the evidence, as it is for so much, is a mixed bag, the stuff we do have tells us a fair bit about the dietary preferences of many Roman soldiers. Sometimes too we can even look in detail at the food produced and stored at individual fortifications. One particularly well-excavated site, which was built and occupied not long before this battle is el-Lejjūn in Jordan (see Image 24). There, excavators found a wide range of potential foods produced and consumed, both locally and regionally. Some of this was meat, with some of the most common consumed on site consisting of chicken, sheep, and goats, which isn't much of a surprise.[69] There's some evidence for wild animals consumed on site too, but we couldn't say who ate them – their proportion of the total is comparatively small. Amongst the fruits, vegetables, and grains, excavators found evidence of wheat and barley, lentils and peas, and then olives, dates, grapes, figs, and peaches.[70]

It wasn't just an issue of collecting food – though this in itself was no mean feat. The Romans expended considerable sums on keeping their soldiers fed. There were officials responsible for collecting it, more forcefully or peaceably, depending on the context. Its preparation seems to have been a task shared by a large number of individuals within a fort like this. While the soldiers are likely to have eaten communal meals in their barracks, it's not always clear if this was solely with other comrades, or with their own family members, or with comrades and recruits. By this stage, the middle of the fourth century CE, lower-ranking Roman soldiers were permitted to marry and have families, something that was frowned upon before though widely practised now.[71] It's possible the women were responsible for much of the food preparation, but it's just as likely to have been the men, who had been doing it for some time in these fortifications.

There's every reason to suppose the soldiers who participated at Strasbourg, at least on the Roman side, had experiences not unlike those who lived at el-Lejjūn, even if their backgrounds were different. Those campaigning with Julian were certainly a different class of soldiers from those in Jordan, but they still likely lived in forts, many with their families. Their diets might have been different – more cattle than sheep and goats, for example – but their food would still have been a mixture of local and regional.

The End – the Water[72]

One last aspect of this battle that manages to convey several sensory experiences is the water that framed the battle. The modern city of Strasbourg sits beside the Rhine, and the mighty river (see Image 25) plays a role in the battle's opening and in its closing. Rivers were a staple of the Roman consciousness, from the Tiber that ran through Rome to the rivers that marked the frontiers, with the Danube, the Rhine, and the Euphrates the most important.[73] The Rhine was where the Romans stopped in Germany. There had been, and would still be, plenty of raids and excursions beyond, though Varus' disaster back in 9 CE was all Augustus needed to stop expansion eastwards. With the Romans on one side and the barbarians on the other, the river marked a fitting barrier (to the Roman) between civilization and barbary. In some ways, then, we could understand this battle, here on the banks of the Rhine, as a fitting location for this struggle between Julian's Romans and the Alamanni's barbarians. But rivers might also have important tactical considerations. There was an entire section of Frontinus' *Stratagems* devoted to rivers.[74] By some reckoning, Hannibal used the Aufidus

River to his own benefit at the Battle of Cannae, which we discussed in Chapter 3.[75] Centuries later, Caesar posted men along the riverbank to harass those who might try to cross. In one of his more famous riverine accomplishments, as he expanded his operations beyond Gaul into Germany, Caesar built and then destroyed a remarkable bridge across the Rhine at Koblenz.[76] Rivers, then, had long played a big role in Roman military matters, battles included.

To get back to Strasbourg, before the battle even begins, in earlier parts of book 16 of the *Res Gestae*, Ammianus draws attention to the importance of the Rhine. When he introduces Julian's achievements, Ammianus notes that

> he vanquished Germany, subdued the meanders of the freezing Rhine, here shed the blood of kings, breathing cruel threats, and there loaded their arms with chains.[77]

This same image, with the Rhine, along with the Euphrates, as a river and land worthy of conquest, returns later in the build-up to Strasbourg.[78] And then later:

> At that same time the savages who had established their homes on our side of the Rhine, were alarmed by the approach of our armies, and some of them skilfully blocked the roads (which are difficult and naturally of heavy grades) by barricades of felled trees of huge size; others, taking possession of the islands which are scattered in numbers along the course of the Rhine, with wild and mournful cries heaped insults upon the Romans and Caesar. Whereupon he was inflamed with a mighty outburst of anger, and in order to catch some of them, asked Barbatio for seven of the ships which he had got ready for building bridges with the intention of crossing the river. but Barbatio burned them all, in order that he might be unable to give any help. Finally, Julian, learning from the report of some scouts just captured, that now in the heat of summer the river could be forded, with words of encouragement sent the light-armed auxiliaries with Bainobaudes, tribune of the Cornuti, to perform a memorable feat, if fortune would favour them; and they, now

wading through the shallows, now swimming on their shields, which they put under them like canoes, came to a neighbouring island and landing there they butchered everyone they found, men and women alike, without distinction of age, like so many sheep. Then, finding some empty boats, they rowed on in these, unsteady as they were, and raided a large number of such places; and when they were sated with slaughter, loaded down with a wealth of booty (a part of which they lost through the force of the current) they all came back safe and sound.[79]

In this long, detailed, and informative passage, the river had served as a means of escape for the Alamanni. Rivers were an important means of getting around in the ancient world, and for many travel by boat was cheaper, quicker, and safer than making a comparable journey by land. The central and lower courses of the Rhine were comparatively easy to travel along.[80] The Rhine is where some of the most spectacular finds of Roman river boats have been recovered, with the majority dating to the fourth century CE.

By the time the battle begins, and Julian gives his speech, one of the things he focuses on is the heat of the day and the lack of water.[81] But he also emboldens his men by reminding them of their earlier success along the Rhine, beyond which the Romans were ranging widely in the lands of the Alamanni.[82] As the two sides move into position, they head towards a gentle hill, not far from the Rhine.[83] So, the river, in Ammianus' telling, plays an important role in the build-up to the meeting of the two sides hand-to-hand.

The river returns, with a vengeance, at the end. As we read earlier in the chapter, near the end the Roman killing of Alamanni was so fierce that their swords were getting blunted from the use, both a visual but also a tactile and auditory experience, with the gleaming, sharp weapons dulled by exertion. At the same time, the bodies of the wounded were getting piled up, so blocking some potential escape routes, which was exacerbated by the location of the Rhine at their backs.[84] Not only is there the sensation of the dulling and slightly pitted swords, but also the closeness and crowding of these increasingly hemmed in warriors, brushing against one another.

Things escalate, and the desperate men try to escape by swimming across the river, much as their countrymen had tried two chapters earlier with some success, though they weren't encumbered by heavy armour. But they sink to the bottom, weighed down by this equipment.[85] This was something men on the opposing side could see, and those on the Alamannic side could almost feel. For Ammianus, this scene was theatrical – a spectacle, of sorts, with the moving back of the curtains revealing some astonishing sights.[86]

> See how some who did not know how to swim clung fast to good swimmers; how others floated like logs when they were left behind by those who swam faster; and some were swept into the currents and swallowed up.[87]

As a former lifeguard myself, I can attest that these kinds of scenes, struggling swimmers climbing all over struggling swimmers in the water, are a lifeguard's worst nightmare. Even experienced swimmers would run into trouble in conditions like this, and it doesn't take much for one struggling swimmer to bring down another, especially when weighed down by heavy, damp clothing and equipment. When you throw in the wounds many would have suffered, the carnage is unsurprising. In fact, for Ammianus, the number of bodies was such that the river was reddened.

Not everyone on the Alamanni side perished, for at least one of the seven kings, Chonodomarius, managed to make it through the piles of bodies and reach his camp. In this case, rather than serve as a hindrance, the river was to help him escape, for boats were beached at the banks ready for use.[88] It didn't go as planned, however:

> he covered his face for fear of being recognized and slowly retired. But when he was already nearing the riverbank and was skirting a lagoon which had been flooded with marsh water, in order to get by, his horse stumbled on the muddy and sticky ground and he was thrown off; but although he was fat and heavy, he quickly escaped to the refuge of a neighbouring hill. But he was recognized (for he could not conceal his identity, being betrayed by the greatness

of his former estate); and immediately a cohort with its tribune followed him with breathless haste and surrounded the wooded height with their troops and cautiously invested it, afraid to break in for fear that some hidden ambush might meet them among the dark shadows of the branches.[89]

Though hardly the noblest of escapes, the scene is full of visual and tactile details. Chonodomarius did his best to escape capture and stayed wary of potential ambushes – enemies he could not see. In his case, then, it was a question of both seeing what threats might be looming, and not being seen himself. This, in turn, applies to the tribune and cohort in pursuit, who were worried about the dark shadows.

Marshes are notoriously difficult to traverse on foot, human or horse, and it's no surprise that they would have tried to skirt the marsh by going around the flooded lagoon. Anyone who's ever tried to wade through marshy, boggy, conditions can attest to the difficulty of passage. Indeed, it's not always possible to gauge the depth of the water, for it's often obscured by both the submergent and emergent vegetation layers. That aside, the footing can be perilous. In other words, it wasn't just a case of a pampered king put off by wet and heavy clothing. No, attempting to cross through the marsh could be his end. To take the wet, muddy, and slippery riverbank might seem a hasty choice, but in this context it makes sense.

Perhaps fittingly, in a battle in which water played an important role, it ended after a trumpet had sounded its conclusion. The Roman soldiers, who had been outnumbered and concerned about Alamannic raids, camped close to the Rhine, near its banks, protected by rows of shields. Importantly, these men who had been hungry and thirsty near the battle's start, now turned to food and drink at its end.[90] Though, at this point in Rome's history, it was still more likely to win than to lose, when we turn to the sixth century in the next chapter, we'll see a world where this wasn't taken for granted, and where the empire's inhabitants were more likely to be on the losing end than the winning one, and we can get a hint of their experiences by looking closer at how the senses influenced their lives in the midst of war.

Ammianus's vivid account provides plenty of insight into the sensory experience of combat in the fourth century CE, both for lower-ranking soldiers and generals. Casting our net wider to include scientific and archaeological data, like human femurs and animal bones, allows us to fill out this discussion. In the end, it's little surprise that pitched battle in close quarters continued to be a sensory overload in the throes of combat.

Chapter 6

The Siege of Edessa (544 CE)

In this last chapter of the book, we come to the end of antiquity
and the reign of Justinian, which is described in considerable
detail by the historian Procopius, and in its pages I explore the
representation and the reality of some of the senses of this siege, like
smell and taste, both items used in unexpected ways. A significant part
of the discussion will focus on the challenges of providing enough food
and drink during a siege, which could impact all classes of resident.
That said, I will also discuss touch, particularly the cramped quarters
that were part of the lived experience in siege mines and countermines.

Sources

Our most important source for this siege is the detailed account
provided by Procopius of Caesarea, a sixth-century CE lawyer and
secretary who spent years in the service of the Empire's then-leading
general, Belisarius.[1] Procopius wrote three works, *The Wars*, a detailed
classicizing account of the wars waged by the emperor Justinian against
the Sasanian Persians (the more specific name for the Persians in this era
of history, owing to the ruling dynasty), the Vandals in North Africa,
and the Ostrogoths in Italy; the *Buildings*, a panegyrical account of
Justinian's building programme, with an especial focus on the work
in Constantinople and the Empire's churches and fortifications; and
the *Secret History*, ostensibly a tell-all account of Justinian's reign that
provides the unadulterated version of why certain individuals acted the
way they did in in the *Wars*.[2]

For the reign and Justinian's wars more generally, there are other
literary sources.[3] Regarding military and political history, we have
the accounts of Agathias and the fragmentary account of Menander
Protector. They provide narratives of the events during Justinian's

reign that Procopius doesn't get to in his *Wars*. Agathias' is rather detailed and only deals with the years from 552 to 558 CE. Menander's picks up after that, but as I say it's only in fragments. They both wrote history in the same manner as Procopius. That is, they wrote classicizing history, history in the style of the classical historians like Herodotus and Thucydides, in Greek, which focussed on political and military affairs and, so far as we can tell (again, Menander's is fragmentary), included some of the same standard features. These include things like descriptions of set-piece or pitched battles, speeches before battle, digressions on foreign peoples and different geographical regions.

There are a host of additional historical sources, however.[4] Malalas wrote his *Chronograph* during the era, which provides a history, of a sort, of the world from creation to the modern day. It includes an historicization of the Trojan War, and some detailed information on some of the big events of Justinian's reign. Marcellinus Comes' *Chronicle* and Jordanes' *Romana* also contain pertinent information. Then there are the law codes, inscriptions, and papyri, all of which, and much more besides, help fill out our understanding of the world of Justinian. Maurice's *Strategikon*, a military manual from around 590 CE, focuses primarily on cavalry, with just one of its twelve books (effectively chapters) on infantry, and another notable one on Rome's enemies.

One type of source which we really do lack, especially regarding this specific siege, is a detailed excavation of the site. The archaeological evidence has the potential to reveal a great deal about siege warfare, and so to compensate for this absence I will rely here on the reports from cities which experienced similar assaults. In particular, I will draw on the earlier, and much better known (archaeologically), 256 CE siege of Dura Europos. That siege, unknown outside of the archaeological record, shared at least one key feature with this siege at Edessa: it too involved the construction of extensive mines and countermines.

Collectively, Procopius' detailed description, combined with the archaeological evidence from the siege of Dura Europos and the assorted additional pieces of evidence, allow us to generate some idea of the sensory experience of the siege of Edessa (see Image 26).

Overview

The Romans and Persians were at war regularly through the course of late antiquity, and after a relative lull in action in the fifth century, things picked up in the sixth. The two superpowers squared off at the century's beginning, with the Sasanians invading Roman territory in modern-day Iraq and reaching the important city of Amida. The lengthy Persian siege is described in detail by the Syriac author, Pseudo-Joshua the Stylite, in his *Chronicle*. Pseudo-Zachariah Rhetor, who wrote an ecclesiastical history (a history of the church, with secular events interspersed), also describes the siege, as does Procopius. Depending on how you understand it, this war continued until 532, after which there was a temporary reprieve that came after the establishment of the poorly named Eternal Peace.[5]

The Siege of Edessa came during the latest outbreak of war, which resumed in 540 CE, when one of the three great cities of the then Empire (along with Constantinople and Alexandria), was sacked by the Persians. A few years later, in the course of another invasion of Roman territory, in 544 CE the Sasanian Persians, led by their king, Khusro, approached the Roman city of Edessa in Mesopotamia and, after seeing their demands for money rejected, began a siege. The sixth-century historian Procopius describes the siege in detail in his *Wars*. Among the highlights are his account of the Persian mound and the attendant mines. First, the Romans built a countermine to try to undermine the Persian mine, which the Persians matched with a countermine of their own. This part of the siege is filled with flames and fires fuelled by a wide variety of materials, so providing a veritable feast for the senses, especially smell. In other contexts, we read about the defenders' use of flammable materials, like olive oil, to toss down onto the Persian attackers approaching on ladders and more. Although olive oil might have been used for cooking food or in its preservation, it was often used as a condiment – in other words, associated with eating and taste, not defence and self-preservation.

The Walls

Quite a lot of the action in the early stages of the siege takes place before the city's walls. While the original walls are no longer extant (so far as I know), there are plenty of comparable, surviving walls from other parts of the region, like those at Diyarbakir, ancient Amida, which are a bit more than a two-hour drive away by car, and which are listed as a UNESCO World Heritage Site (see Image 28).[6] Looking at them gives you a sense of the size and scale of most walls in the sixth-century East. They also illustrate well the difficulty in taking a city surrounded with big, sturdy walls. By starting with walls, we will start with some of the visual features of this siege experience. For the attacker, one of the most notable aspects of these Roman frontier fortresses were their massive walls. Though cities like these had long had walls, a distinctive feature of most Roman fortifications in late antiquity was their imposing size and thickness.[7] In fact, this physical feature of late antique cities was so distinctive that, by the sixth century CE, the century of this siege, walls were recognized by Romans as one of the distinctive features of their cities.[8] So the Persians approaching each and every Roman city would be faced with these imposing edifices. While the seasoned veterans, who had served during several Persian campaigns and so seen many Roman fortresses are less likely to have been intimidated by the sight of these structures, it's hard to imagine that this wouldn't have had an impact on new Persian troops.

The inhabitants, the defenders, would see their walls in another way, perhaps as a source of comfort. When negotiations began between the attacking Persians and the defending Romans, and the Persians were considering abandoning the endeavour, they sent their interpreter, Paul, in front of walls to negotiate terms with the Edessenes.[9] He requested local elites to negotiate, and in response they sent four such men out from the city to the Persian camp to come to some sort of arrangement. This worked out well for both sides: not only could the Persians control the environment by holding the negotiations in their encampment, but the Edessenes could watch it all unfold, from a distance, safely behind their walls.

We don't know the precise route the Persians took in their invasion of Rome, and Procopius or the others don't specify. But, based on the modern topography of Sanliurfa, Turkey, the site of ancient Edessa, the city was surrounded on three sides, the south, west, and north, by hills.[10] It also abutted a river that, though small in many respects, did sometimes flood so causing significant damage, a detail which Procopius himself relates.[11] Owing to this, and Edessa's location vis-à-vis the Persian Empire, the Persians are likely to have approached the city from the southeast (approximately), which was comparatively flat and easy to traverse. Based on this knowledge, the Persians are likely to have constructed their camp in this part of the region too. Procopius says the Persians encamped 7 stades (about 1.29 km) from the city.[12] From their position, the observers on the walls of Edessa would have had a good view of attackers approaching from that direction. Image 29, a snapshot from Google Earth Pro, presupposes that the walls were located somewhere near the current citadel, and observers would have been based somewhere along those walls.[13] If so, we can see their view towards the southeast would have been clear. On the other hand, it's also possible that by putting their camp 7 stades away and in the approximate position where I put them, not only would it be difficult for the Edessenes to get a clear view of Persian preparations, but the landscape might potentially have made it difficult for them to see their army very clearly. The Google Earth Pro view implies that an observer from Edessa at the citadel would not have had a clear sight of the Persian encampment (see Image 29). Of course, this might in part be due to current obstructions (buildings, etc.), but it's interesting nonetheless. View aside, these negotiations failed, and the siege continued.

The Defenders

Defenders in a siege like this took many forms. There were individuals who performed feats of daring, like the general Peter, a leading member of the defence force, who made a sortie from the city's walls with a squadron of Huns.[14] Though we like to think of walls as sometimes impermeable structures, this wasn't always the case. Defenders would often send out mounted raiders with a view to disrupting the efforts of their attackers. In part, the sight of defenders attacking those on the outside seemingly at will could be a means of lowering morale, here of the Persians. This particular sortie worked, because it caught the Persians off guard. Procopius says they killed several Persians, with one man in particular, Argek, killing twenty-seven on his own.[15] On the other hand, despite this initial success, they didn't make any additional sorties, for the Persians were regularly on guard thereafter.

Those posted along the walls would strive to catch the attackers out with a barrage of missiles. While it was unlikely that they would ever fly in sufficient quantity to block out the sun, as was sometimes said to have been the case in pitched battles, the sight of arrows and sound of bullets from slings seem to have been a regular feature of this siege.[16] In a later siege, Procopius describes the efforts of the Persian defenders to push back the Roman besiegers at Petra. They did so by filling pots with sulphur, bitumen, and what he says the Persians called naptha and the Romans 'Medea's oil'.[17] They then poured these on top of the sheds the Romans were bringing to the walls as protection. The sheds themselves were flammable, and these materials were explosive. Once they were set alight, Procopius says, they came close to burning them all. Thanks to the vigorous efforts of the Romans at the side of the shed, the effects were minimal.

One of the most difficult tasks for the attackers was scaling the walls in the first place, and if given the opportunity many an attacking army would bring ladders up against the walls to get inside. We saw this in Chapter 3 at Cartagena. This was always a perilous, even foolhardy, task. To motivate the soldiers, the Romans would give prizes to the first man over, and this seems to have worked in some circumstances. But it didn't always do so. The Persians tried to overcome the impossibility of sneaking the ladders up to the walls in broad daylight by doing so at night. What they didn't bank on, however, was the sound the ladders would make when dozens, even hundreds, were pushed against the walls in the wee hours of the morning.[18] Although, for a time, it seemed to be working, it didn't last long.

As I said earlier, defenders took many forms, and in this story a key role was played by an unidentified peasant. Procopius claims that this guy alone among the Romans was awake, and that at the sound of the ladders he made a great noise to wake up the other defenders. All this might seem surprising – who, after all, had the courage to sleep when their lives seemed to be in the balance in the face of a large Persian host? That they could sleep, however, implies that the defenders at Edessa were a confident bunch. Later we'll look at a major visual, religious explanation for this remarkable sense of calm.

The Siege Mound

One of the more impressive means of scaling the walls of a city was by constructing a siege mound. Indeed, in this very siege, besides the walls, perhaps the most visually striking part of the siege would have been the siege mound the Persians built to effect an entry into the city. After negotiations failed, the Persians started constructing an artificial hill. To make the hill, the Persians cut down lots of trees, and left them laid out in a square. Then they threw in pieces of rocks and earth. All of this would have required a significant physical effort by lots of men.[19] The act of constructing this alone would have been an awesome sight on its own.

To protect from Roman counterattacks, the Persians built goat-fur-covered wooden screens or shields, which Procopius calls *agesta*, though he says they were also called *kilikia*.[20] The Romans weren't sitting idly by, however, for they decided to counter the ever-higher mound by digging a tunnel under the middle of the hill.[21] This structure and its Roman counter have a number of sensory elements. Besides its obvious visual impact, the mine being dug underneath wasn't done in silence. In fact, the construction was loud enough that it gave the Romans away; Procopius even says that the Persians could hear it.[22] This spurred the Persians into further action, and so they built countermines to catch the Romans out, with two constructed aiming to intercept the Romans in the middle.[23] But it gets better. Before we turn to the Roman response to the Persian countermines, I want to jump back to two earlier sieges, which provide some comparative material.

As I noted at the beginning of this chapter, we do have a good deal of comparative material to enhance our understanding of the sensory experience of this siege, and the mound in particular. Before I get to the physical evidence from Dura Europos, I want to go back to Ammianus Marcellinus' detailed description of the siege of Amida in 359 CE. In that famous account, in which Ammianus himself participated, he includes all sorts of personal details that help bring the account alive. In his case, the external siege mound had a pivotal role in the course of the siege, as Ammianus relates:

And the whole space which was between the wall and the external mound being made level as if by a causeway or a bridge, opened a passage to the enemy, which was no longer embarrassed by any obstacles; and numbers of our men, being crushed or enfeebled by their wounds, gave up the struggle. Still men flocked from all quarters to repel so imminent a danger, but from their eager haste they got in one another's way, while the boldness of the enemy increased with their success. By the command of the king all his troops now hastened into action, and a hand-to-hand engagement ensued. Blood ran down from the vast slaughter on both sides: the ditches were filled with corpses, and thus a wider path was opened for the besiegers. And the city, being now filled with the eager crowd which forced its way in, all hope of defence or of escape was cut off, and armed and unarmed without any distinction of age or sex were slaughtered like sheep.[24]

In that episode we can see how important a mound could be. It conveys too some of the fear that participants might have felt at the unfolding events. One of the senses we can see particularly prominently in that description is touch, with some soldiers crushed by the stampede of their comrades.

The remains of Dura allow us to appreciate the sensation of a siege mound from the inside.[25] Dura Europos was a Macedonian settlement, founded in the decades after Alexander's death and in the wake of the wars of his successors (*diadochi*). Later, the Parthians superseded the Seleucids and took the town, and later still it became Roman in the 160s CE, which is what it was in 256 CE, when the Sasanian Persians came a-calling. By some accounts, the northwest sector of the city was militarized. But it wasn't just filled with soldiers, for there were plenty of additional buildings, like an amphitheatre and some baths. After the Persians took the city in 256, Dura was abandoned and never inhabited again, which is why its remains were fairly well preserved (until Daesh/Isis/Isil caused some destruction). Its plentiful body of evidence includes beautiful frescoes, pieces of military equipment, graffiti, papyri, much of the settlement's physical structures, and the remains of some dead soldiers.²⁶ The story of the dead soldiers goes something like this.

A few months into a siege that had so far achieved mixed results, the Sasanid Persians decided to try something new to gain entry of the Roman-controlled city, Dura Europos, in what is today Syria. The Persians had already made vigorous attempts at the southern end of the city, constructing a siege ramp, tunnels, and countermines. But now they shifted to the western boundary. Near Tower 19 at the western edge of the city's walls, the Persians started tunnelling a mine. Working tirelessly and starting some 30–40 metres out from the tower, the Persians finally started to make some headway, and they were probably hopeful that their efforts would lead to the undermining of the wall and the effecting of an entrance into the city. All this digging didn't go unnoticed by the Romans, however, probably because of the noise itself and the growing mound of debris comprised material from the hole. In response, the Romans started constructing a countermine of their own.

This siege hadn't caught the Romans unaware. A few decades earlier, the Sasanids had usurped the Persian throne from the Arsacids, who had ruled the Persian Empire (known as the Parthian Empire) for a few centuries. Riding the coat-tails of the victories of Ardashir, the Sasanid dynasty's first ruler, who had achieved considerable success in the 220s CE in Mesopotamia (roughly modern Iraq between the Tigris and Euphrates rivers), the Persians had invaded Rome's eastern frontier in the 230s. Under a new king, Shapur I (the Great), the Persians had surged across into Roman territory. In response, the then Roman emperor, Gordian III, opened the doors of Janus in Rome and sent a massive army that pushed deep into Persian territory. It didn't go as planned, however, and the Persians defeated and killed Gordian in battle in early 244 CE. Nearly a decade later, Shapur I and the Persians again threatened Roman territory, sacking the major city of Antioch (in modern Turkey) in the early 250s CE. The current Roman emperor, Valerian, brought a large army of his own in 254 or 255, and sought to repel the invaders.

All of these events and more besides provided the Romans living on the frontier with plenty of exposure to the challenging geo-political situation. It also likely spurred on some Roman cities to shore up their defences in the event of a new Persian invasion. Dura Europos was one such city. At some point in the years leading up to 256 CE, the Romans reinforced their city by constructing anti-siege ramparts abutting the walls, which covered three of the city's four sides (the fourth laying on the River Euphrates). This might have been done in advance of the city's first siege at the hands of the Persians at some point between 252 and 254 CE, or more likely in advance and in light of the second and final siege which began in 254 or 255. While these stronger defences did enable the city to hold out against the Persians for a year or two, ultimately, it was unsuccessful.

And so, at some point before the fall of Dura in 256 CE, the Persians built a mine, which was opposed by a Roman countermine. This came at the same time that the Persians were making an attempt on a number of the city's gates. Amongst the many Roman defenders involved in the defence of the city through this mine, some probably had names like Aelius Bassus, Aurelius Cassianus, Appadana Iulius Crispinus, Theobolus Gaddes, and Magdala Aurelius Germanus. Eventually the countermine had managed to come within reach of the Persian mine, and the Romans prepared for an assault. So, those five men and several others, fully armed and holding their most recent pay cheques (bags of coins), prepared to charge the Persians and halt the advance, at least at this one spot. Unfortunately for their sakes, the Persians weren't caught unawares. The Persians learned of the Roman countermine and took appropriate action, which took the form of a chemical attack: using some sort of device to generate smoke, the Persians unleashed naphtha and sulphur into the Roman mine. All those Roman soldiers, Aelius Bassus and others, were overcome by the fumes and died where they stood, still fully armed. Once the smoke had cleared, the Persians entered the Roman tunnel, and threw the bodies into a pile. They also brought in some flammable materials to bring down the countermine. When the bodies had been piled up and the fire was ready to go, one unfortunate Persian soldier, still armed, was tasked with setting it alight. Although he completed his task, he didn't get out in time and instead perished, only to be rediscovered, centuries later, along with the Romans.

Nineteen Roman soldiers and one Sasanian soldier became entombed in a mine near Tower 19 of Dura Europos, Syria (see Image 30 for an illustration). These remains are some of the most remarkable battlefield finds ever found from the Roman world. We don't know the names of the deceased, but it's easy to imagine who they might have been thanks to the survival of detailed military rosters from that same site, only dated a few decades earlier. One, P. Dur. 101 (=RMR 2) is dated as late as 222 CE and includes the names of many hundreds of soldiers. Although few if any of these are likely to have been serving at Dura more than twenty-five years later when the Persians besieged the city, it's easy to imagine similarly named individuals buried in the mine to those listed on the roster – and this is where the names mentioned above were drawn. The names lend the Roman dead more humanity than they might otherwise have had; that we have bodies too only brings this out even more.

That mound at Dura allows us to visualize, with greater clarity, the mound and mines at Edessa. Back at Edessa, to counter the Persian countermines, the Romans acted swiftly and decisively. According to Procopius:

> the Romans discovered this and abandoned the attempt, throwing earth into the place that had been hollowed out, and then began to work on the lower part of the mound at the end of it that was next to the wall, and by taking out timbers, stones, and earth, they opened a space like a chamber; then they threw in there dry trunks of trees that burn most easily, saturated them with cedar oil, and added much sulphur and bitumen.[27]

They didn't start the fires just yet, but they were ready to go, just in case the siege negotiations, at this point still ongoing, broke down – and they did.

At this stage, the Romans set fire to the trees. Unfortunately, the trees would burn out so they had to continuously add new fuel, more wood, to keep the fire going. The fire itself, once started, was impressive enough that it could be seen from all parts of this significant hill. But it wasn't the flames so much as the smoke.[28] To expand the fire, the

Romans threw small pots with coal and fire to all parts of the hill, and as Persians rushed to put those out, they assumed that's where the smoke was coming from. The smell and sight of the smoke, let alone its taste, had an impact on the initially unsuspecting Persians.

The action continued. Khusro arrived with the bulk of his army, and he managed to figure out where the smoke was coming from. So, he ordered the Persians to start throwing earth and water on those spots where smoke was seen rising. Though this worked for a time, eventually smoke would pop up somewhere else.[29] To make matters worse, the water poured on the smoke only seemed to animate the bitumen and sulphur and to really make the wood burn; eventually the smoke was so thick that you could see it from some distance, nearly 37 km away at Carrhae, the site of Crassus' famous defeat, modern Harran (see Image 31).[30] Eventually, the Persians gave up on the mound. The seemingly endless smelling and tasting of the smoke billowing from the mound are likely to have had a significant impact on the ability of those many Persians manning the mound to continue their efforts, especially if, as Procopius would have us believe, their considerable efforts to temper the flames proved fruitless. So although those inside the Roman mine would have had to contend with dark and close quarters, so testing their tolerance to the touch (and maybe, due to exertion, the smell) of their comrades, it wasn't for naught.

An (Un)expected Sight

The last significant sensory aspect of this siege comes from the religious sphere, and it's something with a long tradition. The narrative of the siege, thus far, has relied primarily on the account of Procopius. But it's not the only one. One later version comes via Evagrius Scholasticus, who wrote an ecclesiastical history of his day that meshed the religious with the secular. He used Procopius as a source (he even quoted him) for some of the events that he describes; but sometimes he goes beyond the historian from Caesarea. One such case is here, when he claims that the residents of Edessa were aided in their defence by something sometimes called the mandylion, an image of Jesus Christ on a piece of cloth, the first icon (see Image 32). According to him, thanks to the earlier King Abgar's communications with Jesus, Edessa was said to never come under enemy control.[31] This power, from Christ, was transmitted to the city by means of a letter, which Eusebius reported verbatim.[32] For Procopius, this letter gave the Edessenes confidence during an earlier invasion by Khusro I, in 540 CE.[33] But power also came from the aforementioned mandylion.

Its use, first recorded here in this story, goes back to the siege mound.[34] According to Evagrius, after the Romans had constructed their countermine, they started putting wood in with a view to setting it alight. In Evagrius' version, the fire wouldn't start. This was because it lacked oxygen – Evagrius says something to this effect. This brought the Edessenes to a state of despair. So, in desperation, they went and fetched the mandylion. In Evagrius' words, 'they brought the divinely created image, which human hands had not made, the one that Christ the God sent to Abgar when he yearned to see Him'.[35] They brought it inside, sprinkled it with water, and then put some of this on the pyre. Surprise, surprise, the wood caught fire. At this point, Evagrius returns, more or less, to Procopius' version (which didn't mention the trouble with starting the fire). The fire works, and the Persians withdraw, all down to this holiest of sights. Let alone whether there was such an item, whether it was the image of Christ or not, its visual impact was marked. Seeing this image gave the Edessenes the morale boost they needed to carry out their task.

Although it's no big surprise that Evagrius put so much stock in the role of this icon in changing the course of the siege, it's worth drawing attention to Procopius too, a fellow Christian, for he too is not opposed to providing religious explanations for the outcomes of battles and sieges.[36] Another siege that he described in great detail was the siege of Antioch, which took place in 540 CE. His explanation for that siege – the Persians sacked this important Roman city – is religious in character. In a nutshell, by his reckoning, Antioch was sacked by the immorality of the people, whom God sought to punish.[37] Procopius frames his account of Edessa in a similar way: his description begins with some comments about the supposed religious nature of Khusro's campaigns in the 540s.[38] A few chapters earlier, he highlights the piety of the Edessenes, who weren't likely to suffer in the same way as the

Antiochenes.[39] Before the heart of the action kicks off, he notes that Khusro saw some sort of vision.[40] It seems to me, then, that Procopius tried to say that religious visions played some sort of role in the siege without explicitly saying so, and that by doing so he was making subtle allusions to the icon. To understand this siege, from the perspective of most Romans in the sixth-century Empire and an even higher proportion of the Edessenes, it's important to consider the hand of God, lurking behind many (if not all) things, and which was often manifest in terms of visual things, like visions and icons.

Smelling and Tasting

But it wasn't just a case of what you could see at this siege, but also what you could smell and taste, something I touched on earlier. Near the beginning of his description of the siege, Procopius notes the preparations, including the seizing of flocks of animals to bring into the city, so inhabitants could have stuff to eat during its peak.[41] Keeping the defenders well fed and watered was always one of the most significant challenges during a siege, much as we saw in Chapter 4 above at Masada. The situation here is no different. Though Procopius' account implies that they brought in some significant supplies of food, and as we already know there was a small river that ran through the town, the latter, at least, seems to have been inconsistent in terms of its flow. Procopius himself says it provided the city with ample water, but also knows that it could become problematic. The historian also claims that some years before this siege, Justinian went to some trouble to shore up the city's water supply, though his account here is problematic.[42] At the very least, if this happened, this would have given the defenders one less thing to worry about. All this said, it's worth stressing that sufficient food and water wouldn't only be a problem for the defenders, but also the attackers. Too much time spent in one area could deplete local resources.

The defenders would have employed a variety of devices to defend themselves against the Persian attack, and in this siege like many others, these defenders would have comprised men and women of a variety of ages and classes. Sieges were one of the forms of combat from the ancient Mediterranean world in which women played an important and manifest role. Although we find women regularly depicted in ancient mythical combat, pitched battles included, this is less the case in narrative historical accounts. For instance, the most famed groups of warrior women from antiquity were the Amazons, who have been the subject of a lot of attention.[43] Famously, from the Trojan War, Penthesileia and her Amazon army show up at Troy after the events in the *Iliad* in support of their allies, the Trojans. When they finally face battle with the Greeks, they fare well, but their queen, the aforementioned Penthesileia, comes face-to-face with Achilles, the greatest of Greek warriors, who is all but invincible. The two clash, but he wins, and in the process strikes the fatal blow. In some accounts, once Achilles caught sight of Penthesileia, he was smitten, although it was already too late (she was dead or dying).

While we have no direct evidence for Amazons from myth quite like Penthesileia, that's not to say there isn't evidence of women warriors. Graves do exist, and they're found in and around the Eurasian steppes.[44] But women are never found serving in Roman armies, whether earlier or later, even if they were an integral part of the wider Roman military community.[45] They do surface regularly, however, in the context of sieges, as here. In cases like this, it was a matter of expediency. Procopius himself says that the Edessenes were outnumbered by the Persians by some measure.[46] There weren't enough soldiers and so women and children – Procopius doesn't say how old they were – stepped up, moving to the walls to defend their city. According to Procopius, 'meanwhile, the women, children, and aged also were gathering stones for the fighters and assisting them in other ways'.[47]

Edessa wasn't unusual in this regard, for there was a whole history of women in Eastern cities working feverishly to defend their cities in any way they could. At Amida, which was besieged in 502–503 CE by the Persians, the civilian inhabitants there played a big role. After a significant sortie carried out by Roman soldiers, Pseudo-Joshua the Stylite noted that 'women carried water and took it outside the wall for the fighters to drink'.[48] Procopius' account of the women at this same siege differs in significant ways. According to him, at a point in the siege when Kavad and the Persians were thinking of abandoning the siege, 'some courtesans shamelessly drew up their clothing and displayed to Kavad, who was standing close by, those parts of a woman's body that it is not proper for men to see uncovered.'[49] Though this isn't necessarily the same group, that he highlights this and not the giving of water is significant: his literary aims differed markedly from Pseudo-Joshua. For our purposes, Pseudo-Joshua's observation is more valuable.

Providing food and water wasn't the only way women might contribute to the defence of their cities. One of the most common and accessible ways to defend a city from its walls was by using olive oil, and Procopius says it was some women in the city who used it to defend its walls.[50] He says that the olive oil would be heated and then poured down on people. Olive oil was grown and produced across the Mediterranean in the classical period, and late antiquity was no different. There's evidence for olive oil presses in villages all over the eastern Mediterranean, the core of the Roman Empire in the sixth century. Local ones are likely to have been the source for the olive oil used here. Usually, of course, olive oil was a staple of the Mediterranean diet, and so its use was saved for meals, though it was also often used as a fuel for lamps. The oil was used for machines and for food all over northern Mesopotamia, where Edessa was. It was used as a cooking fat and a condiment. It could also be used to help preserve certain foods. But desperate times call for desperate measures, and its use as a fuel could be put to full advantage in cases like this.

Now olive oil was only one of the more unusual items defenders might use in defence of their cities. Here, at Edessa, we find other things too, like bitumen and sulphur. Bitumen, what we usually think of as oil, has a powerful, and for many (most?) an unpleasant smell. The smell of this burning would have been potent. But so too the use of sulphur, which is famous for its horrible, rotten egg smell. The use of these, deep in the Roman countermine, would have made the working conditions challenging for the soldiers entrusted with the task of setting all of this on fire. On the other hand, though the cedar oil would also, presumably, have helped the wood catch on fire, it likely would have had a far more pleasant smell, at least if it smelled anything like cedar wood. Desperate times called for desperate measures, and those called to defend their homes would use any means at their disposal to do so.

Given olive oil's ubiquity, it's no surprise that it was used here – and though Procopius (and others) might not say much about its role as a defensive tool in other operations, this doesn't mean it wasn't used.

In Chapter 2, at the end I noted some possible parallels between the Battle of Vicksburg during the US Civil War and the siege of Rome in 537/538 CE. In those two sieges, the respective commanders on the defensive, Penderton at Vicksburg and Bessas at Rome, who had ready access to supplies, hoarded food at the expense of the cities they were defending for their own personal gain. Bessas' case is worth highlighting for this was a real possibility during any siege, especially one in which the defenders got desperate.

As we saw in Chapter 4, food security was a big issue during sieges, and this one was no exception. Yet, as detailed as the account of Edessa is, even more extraordinary is Procopius' account of the siege of Rome in 537/538. In that case, the Romans (i.e. East Romans) along with the residents of the city were on the defensive against the besieging Goths. Belisarius played a pivotal role in the siege's success and the Roman survival. Eventually he moved on and seemingly won the war before heading back to Constantinople. When he returned sometime later, Bessas was in charge at Rome. This isn't a surprise, for the aged general appears throughout Procopius' *Wars*, and plays an important role in a variety of episodes. He often dutifully performs the tasks that Procopius assigns him.[51] Though this should have been an opportunity for Bessas to improve his already good position in Rome and his reputation amongst the Roman high command, instead he saw it as an opportunity to prosper.[52] When Rome was later besieged again by the Goths in the 540s, it was Bessas who was in command of the garrison. Food supplies became strained and though there might well have been enough for all, the elderly general (he had started serving in around 503) started hoarding the goods for personal gain.[53] And, as the siege continued, famine grew in the city, eventually gripping the populace.

But the famine became more severe and was greatly increasing its wasting effects, driving men to discover monstrous foods unknown to human nature. Now at first, Bessas and Conon, who commanded the garrison in Rome, had, as it happened, stored away a vast supply of grain for their own use within the walls of Rome, and they as well as the soldiers were taking from the portion assigned for their own needs and selling it at great prices to the Romans who were rich; for the price of a *medimnos* had reached seven gold pieces. But people whose private circumstances were such that they could not obtain food that was so expensive, were able, by paying one-fourth of this price, to have their *medimnoi* filled with bran; they ate this and necessity made it most sweet and tender. As for beef, whenever the guardsmen of Bessas captured an ox in making a sally, they sold it for fifty gold pieces. And if any man had a horse or other animal that died, this Roman was counted among those extremely fortunate, as he was able to live luxuriously upon the flesh of a dead animal. But all the rest of the populace were eating nettles only, which grow in abundance about the walls and among the ruins in all parts of the city. In order to prevent the coarse herb from stinging their lips and throat they boiled them thoroughly before eating. So long, then, as the Romans had gold coins, they bought their grain and bran in the manner described and went on their way; but when their supply of this had at length failed, then they brought all their household goods to the forum and exchanged them for their daily sustenance. But when, finally, the soldiers of the emperor had no grain that they could possibly sell to the Romans (except a little that Bessas still had left), nor did the Romans have anything left with which to buy, they all turned to the nettles. But this food was insufficient for them, for it was impossible to satisfy themselves on it and consequently their flesh withered away almost entirely, while their colour, gradually turning to a livid hue, made them look like images of themselves. It happened to many that, even as they were walking along chewing the nettles with their teeth, death came suddenly upon them and they fell to the ground. They were already beginning to eat each other's dung. There were many too who, pressed by the famine, killed themselves with their own hands, for they could no longer find either dogs or mice or any dead animal of any kind on which to feed. There was a

Roman in the city, the father of five children; and they gathered around him and, clutching at his clothes, kept demanding food. But he, without a word of lament and without any sign that he was disturbed, but most steadfastly concealing all his suffering in his mind, told the children to follow him as if to get food.[54]

These were the conditions in Rome. Food was scarce and the residents suffered in these truly horrid conditions. Where we might hope that Bessas would step up and provide some relief, he did not.

For now he [Bessas] was the only one who still had any grain left, as of all the grain that the magistrates of Sicily had previously sent to Rome to suffice both for the soldiers and the whole population, he had let an extremely small amount go to the populace while he kept for himself the largest part on the pretext of providing for the soldiers and had hidden it away; as he was selling this to the senators at high prices, he did not wish the siege to be broken.[55]

Bessas acted like a late antique Penderton at Vicksburg, and Rome, the eternal city, suffered as a result. The population of the capital seems to have shrunk significantly over the course of the sixth century CE with first this protracted war with the Goths and later the wars with the Lombards the cause of all the city's misfortune. Although Procopius doesn't tell us about the condition of the food, it's also possible that what little they had would have spoiled, or at least some of it did, as seems to have been the case at Masada.

Ultimately, tasting and smelling were all-pervasive aspects of the experience of battle at Edessa in 544, much as they would be in most sieges from the ancient Mediterranean world. This was particularly true of the civilians who often were called on to fight in the direst of circumstances – and who often suffered the worst when things went wrong, as they often did. They likely saw and heard horrible things – and they might even have had to touch uncomfortable things, like dead bodies, dirty tools, and rotten food. But so much went back to the basics, like eating and drinking, where taste and smell were everything.

Wrapping Up

The Siege of Edessa was a feast for the senses, and though we've covered a great deal, there is plenty more I could have discussed. For instance, I could have discussed the place of animals in these sieges, at least more directly. Along those lines, there's a reference to an elephant brought to the walls in this siege in a much later part of the narrative. In that later account, Procopius says the Persians brought an elephant up to the walls with a view to using its platform to shoot at the defenders at the walls. The attack, from the Persian perspective, seemed to be going well, for Procopius claims that they were on the verge of overpowering men on the tower at that point.[56] But the Romans knew what to do, and dangled a pig before the walls in front of the elephant. The pig, unsurprisingly, squealed, and both the sight and sound of the pig was enough to make the elephant turn around and leave the wall. The elephant wasn't just put off by the pig but legitimately scared, for Procopius says it 'got out of control' and stepped back, little by little, from the fortifications.[57] In this case, the experience of the animals was part of the larger sensory experience of this battle, which could be all encompassing, as it was here at Edessa.

Conclusion

I've now reached the end of this short book. In the preceding pages, we've gone from Cunaxa and the lifetime of Xenophon to Edessa and Procopius. Though those two places, Cunaxa and Edessa, are in geographic terms quite close, chronologically and, to some degree, culturally, a great deal separates the two. Four of the six chapters focused on pitched battles between two opposing armies, two in Europe and two in Asia. Although the Greeks and Romans, broadly speaking, were the focus of most of the attention, they weren't always the victors. The other participants were from diverse places that ranged from central Europe to North Africa and off to central Asia – Alamanni, Carthaginians, and Persians. I tried, too, to look at the experiences of individuals across the social spectrum from the ancient Mediterranean world. While that, of necessity, means a lot of men, many of whom would have had better lives than many of their contemporaries, the life of a general was quite different from that of a lowly grunt.

I also tried to incorporate, where possible, as much of the lived sensory experiences of those from the margins of that ancient Mediterranean world, particularly the women and children who so often suffer the most in war. The aim wasn't only to add variety to the subject matter, but also to illustrate how the senses are experienced by different groups in different ways. Though some, like taste and smell, can be associated with an overall levelling of social levels in the middle of a siege, it's also true that the visual experience of a soldier in the middle of a pitched battle, particularly an infantry soldier on the Roman side at Cannae or a Roman defender in a mine at Edessa, is quite different from that of a commander-in-chief, like Alexander at Issus. The soldiers' perspectives would have been limited to their immediate environs. There was only so much they could hope to see. This could lead to fear, particularly if they were new recruits unfamiliar with battle. To counter this, some armies seem to have tried to modify their order of battle accordingly. On the other hand, the position of a general like Alexander was determined, to a large degree, by maximizing what he could see in a battle of his own – the more, the merrier, at least if he was to manage battle effectively. A general who couldn't see what was going on couldn't change tactics on the fly (as much as that was possible).

As I said, one significant group of people whom I turned to in at least two chapters, 4 and 6, which dealt with sieges, were the women and children. Indeed, one of the great benefits of sensory history is that it allows us to get at the experiences, as best we can, of those who have left behind little or no trace in the traditional pieces of evidence – the literary histories and, at least as far as warfare is concerned, the inscriptions (though there are exceptions). Our literary record was composed almost entirely by male authors, and elite ones at that. Their interests are those of their peers and predecessors. They often care little, if at all, for those beneath them. But by bringing in the abundant additional pieces of data we can look into all these other groups. Though I spent some time on women and occasionally referred to children, there is plenty more to be said. Then there are all those other groups – the conquered, the slaves, and more – whom I didn't mention.

Although aspects of the sensory approach share a lot with the face-of-battle approach, I hope I've demonstrated that the sensory approach has the potential to take things a bit further, and that it involves a potentially greater collection of individuals. By incorporating all the (common) senses, there is more potential for engagement with, and investigation into, each battle and siege. Just as important, the explanatory potential is greater, or so it seems to me.

Fortunately, for all the limitations of our sources, there is quite a lot we can say. In fact, in this book I hope that I've only scratched the surface. For one thing, I've talked more about Rome than Greece. The starting point too was comparatively late. I all but left off Archaic Greece, to say nothing of the Bronze Age, or the armies and warfare of all those Middle Eastern kingdoms and empires, like the Hittites and Neo-Assyrians. Different peoples and different ages aside, there are plenty of other battles and sieges from the ancient Mediterranean world within the timeframe I did choose, about 400 BCE to 550 CE, about which we are well informed. To give just a few examples, the aforementioned Battle of the Teutoburg Forest (9 CE), the Battle of Marathon (490 BCE), the Battle of Chaeronea (338 BCE), the Siege of Alesia (52 BCE), the Siege of Amida (359 CE), and the Siege of Rome (537/538 CE), to name but a few. Works on individual wars or specific types of individuals (like legionaries) would also be welcome. Even those specific battles and sieges that I focused on here could do with much more detailed investigation. Plus, I've said almost nothing about guerrilla warfare, asymmetric combat, and battles at sea. In short, there is no shortage of potential topics that could adopt this approach – and do a far better job than I have!

Sensory history can be both evocative and interpretive, even when applied to military topics. In certain circumstances you could make a case that the senses influence behaviour, as I suggested at various points in this book. As we've seen, different groups don't all experience senses in the same way, so contextualization is important. Ultimately, thinking about sensory experience among ancient combatants can help bring to light something of the lives of the silent majority, and the levelling impact of ancient combat when Mars is shaking his spear.

Notes and References

Introduction

1. For an engaging account of the battle, see Murdoch (2008). Wells (2003: 177–185) too gets into the experience of this battle at the end, in a chapter entitled 'The Killing Zone', which seems to consciously imitate a similarly named paper by Lazenby (1991) on Greek warfare.
2. Cass. Dio, 56.20, trans. Cary.
3. Cass. Dio, 56.21.2–4, trans. Cary.
4. On the discovery, see Clunn (2005). For the battle, see Murdoch (2008), mentioned above, and Wells (2003).
5. Wells (2003).
6. Wells (2003), p. 164.
7. Wells 2003, p. 101.
8. Murdoch (2008).
9. Wells (2003), p. 52.
10. Caes. *BG*. 5.44.
11. Murdoch (2008) (I accessed this book via kindle, so see location 2491 of 4280 for more on this).
12. Hom. *Il*. 4.494ff., trans. Murray.
13. Thuc. 7.44.1.
14. Greenwood 2006: 36.
15. Synott (1991), p. 63; Smith (2007), p. 28.
16. Rutherford (2004); Smith (2010); Hamilakis (2013), p. 24–6.
17. Aristotle, *On the Soul* 3.435a, 13–14.
18. Squire (2016b).
19. See for example, Procop. *Wars* 1.18.31, 5.27.16, 7.4.29.
20. Procop. *Wars* 7.1.8.
21. Procop. *Buildings* 1.2.5–12, 1.10.16; Corippus, *In laudem Iustini minoris* 3.120–25.
22. Smith (2015), pp. 39–65.
23. Daly (2000); Goldsworthy (1996); Hanson (1989); Matthew (2015).
24. Smith (2015).
25. Hamilakis (2013); Butler and Purves (2014); Bradley (2014); Squire (2016).
26. Hanson (1989); Goldsworthy (1997); Lenski (2007).
27. Smith (2003).
28. Hanson (1989); Goldsworthy (1997); Daly (2000); Lenski (2007).

Chapter 1: The Battle of Cunaxa (401 BCE)

1. It can be found at 1.8 of Xenophon's *Anabasis*, which is widely available in translation.
2. For a concise account of the battle, see Trundle (2017), pp. 412–13.
3. See the helpful, short, list in Rop (2019), p 33.
4. For instance, the title to Fox's (2004) insightful edited volume is *The Long March. Xenophon and the Ten Thousand*.
5. Flower (2012); Rop (2019).
6. Rop (2019), pp 32–8.
7. Xen. *Anab*. 1.7.11.
8. Diod. Sic. 14.22.2.
9. Stylianou (2004), pp 91–2.
10. Plut. *Artax*. 7–13.
11. Liston (2020).
12. For an excellent introduction to Greek warfare, see Sears (2019).
13. One of the more stirring, though now hotly-debated, accounts of hoplite warfare is Hanson's (1989).
14. For a neat summary, see Hunt (2007).
15. Sekunda (2007).
16. Bugh (2006).
17. Konijendijk (2018).
18. Hanson (1989), p 16.
19. Konijendijk (2018).
20. Echeverría (2012).
21. Hanson (1989), pp 28–9.
22. See Van Wees (2004), pp 185–7.
23. Though older, a sensible and balanced account of the issue comes from Krentz (1985), who also wrote an engaging book on similar issues, though centred on the Battle of Marathon (Krentz, 2010).
24. Konijnendijk (2018).
25. Rop (2019).
26. Xen. *Anab*. 1.8, trans. Waterfield.
27. There has been quite a lot of work on speeches, including a spirited debate about their historicity with some significant articles by Hansen (1993, 2001), Pritchett (1994, 2002), and Anson (2010).
28. Xen. *Ag*. 2.12, trans. Marchant.
29. Konijnendijk (2018), p 140.
30. Hdt. 9.54.2—56.1
31. Plut. *Lyc*. 22.2–3; Wheeler (2007), p 204.
32. Van Wees (2004), p 186.
33. This point comes courtesy of Waterfield in his translation.
34. Xen. *Anab*. 1.8.18.

35. For a detailed discussion of the war cry, see Gersbach (2020), who instead uses the term 'battle expression', which in turn encompasses a much broader range of activities.
36. Xen. *Anab.* 1.7.4, trans. Waterfield.
37. See Xen. *Anab.* 1.8.16–19.
38. Plut. *Lyc.* 6.5.
39. Plut. *Lyc.* 21.4.
40. Plut. *Lyc.* 22.2–3, trans. Perrin.
41. Plut. *Lyc.* 22.1–2, trans. Perrin.
42. Xen. *Hel.* 3.1.1. See too Rop (2019), pp 79–84.
43. The figures come from Wikipedia's data for Baghdad. Cunaxa is believed to have been quite close to Baghdad, some the information is likely fairly accurate, or at least representative and illustrative. https://en.wikipedia.org/wiki/Baghdad#Climate. Accessed July 14, 2020.
44. Xen. *Anab.* 1.8.20.
45. Xen. *Anab.* 1.8.20.
46. Xen. *Anab.* 1.8.21–22.
47. For Xenophon's overstated claims, see Rop (2019) pp 30–63. For the army as a respectable fighting force, see Whitby (2004).
48. Whitby (2004), p 225.
49. Plut. *Artax.* 8.3–7; Whitby (2004), pp 226–7.
50. Trundle (2017), p 413.
51. Echeverría (2012), p 307.
52. Thuc. 5.71. Trans. Dutton.
53. Echeverría (2011), p 62.
54. Details and references at Echeverría (2012), p 305.
55. Echeverría (2011).
56. See the description in Krentz (2010), pp 46–50
57. Krentz (1985), p 53.
58. Krentz (2010), p 50.
59. For a clear and concise discussion, see Schwartz (2013). For more detail, see his book: Schwartz (2009), pp 25–54.
60. Schwartz (2013) p 158.
61. Schwartz (2013), p 161.
62. Lee (2007).
63. Lee (2007), pp 120–121.
64. Lee (2007), p 208.
65. Xen. *Anab.* 4.3.10, trans. Waterfield.
66. Lee (2007), pp 220.
67. Xen. *Anab.* 4.1.8.
68. Xen. *Anab.* 4.2.22.
69. Xen. *Anab.* 4.4.9.
70. Xen. *Anab.* 4.5.7–8, trans. Waterfield.

71. A related issue was the production of waste, which comes with all eating and drinking. A big, potentially smelly issue for a large group like this was what to do with all that waste, and how do you prevent it from becoming a hazard. See Lee (2007), pp 236–8.

Chapter 2: The Battle of Issus (333 BCE)
1. Bugh (2006).
2. Bosworth (1988).
3. Wheeler (1991).
4. Lendon (2005), p 128.
5. Note the comments of Heckel (2008), p 27.
6. Sabin (2007) notes that the battle is hard to reconstruct because of all the divergent accounts. Though we know it was at the ancient Pinarus River, we don't know which modern one corresponds to it – and there is much scholarly disagreement.
7. Worthington (2017), p 529.
8. Justin's (11.9.1–10), for instance, is only a few lines, and he gives no indication of how the battle unfolded beyond the wounding of Alexander and Darius.
9. Polyb. 12.20.7, trans. Cary.
10. Polyb. 20.18.3, trans. Cary.
11. Iustin. 11.9.1–10. Justin, Quintus Curtius, Diodorus, Plutarch, and Arrian also describe this battle.
12. Curt. 3.7–11.
13. Curt. 3.8.18–20.
14. Curt. 3.8.10, 3.8.15, 3.8.26, 3.8.30, 3.9.11, 3.10.1, and esp. 3.11.11ff.
15. Diod. 17.32.4–37.
16. Diod. 17.32.6–7, trans. Oldfather. Diodorus here follows Lucian's precepts by describing the action as something of a balancing act between the two forces.
17. Plut. *Alex.* 20.1–5.
18. Arrian, 2.6.6, trans. Brunt.
19. Arrian, 2.7.3–4.
20. Arrian 2.9.3.-4, trans. Brunt.
21. Arrian 2.10.6, trans. Brunt.
22. Sabin (2007).
23. Heckel (2008).
24. Bugh (2006).
25. See Cuomo (2007), p 41–76.
26. Brice (2011).
27. Sekunda (2007). Lendon (2005) argued that Homer was the direct inspiration for Philip's new phalanx.
28. Sekunda (2007).

29. Lendon (2005).
30. Heckel (2008).
31. Sekunda (2007).
32. Strauss (2006). On Macedonian combined arms, see Wrightson (2019), pp 159–215.
33. Lendon (2005).
34. Wheeler (2007).
35. Lendon (2005), p 128.
36. Bosworth (1988).
37. Bosworth (1988), pp 266 and 271. See also Heckel (2008)
38. Heckel (2008).
39. Heckel (2008), pp 27–8.
40. Lendon (2005), p 129.
41. Quint. Curt. 7.6.26, trans Rolfe.
42. More recently, some have argued for a world and way of war that emphasized both competition and cooperation. See Varto (forthcoming).
43. Note Van Wees (1988, 1992, 1994, 1996), and Snodgrass (2013).
44. Plut. *Alex.* 15.7–9, trans. Perrin.
45. Much of this stems from Wheeler (1991, 2007). For a succinct overview, see Moore (2013).
46. See Wheeler (2001) for instance.
47. Wrighston (2019).
48. Wrightson (2019).
49. Arr. *Anab.* 1.13.4–5. Matthew (2015), p 335.
50. Arr. *Anab.* 2.10.5.
51. Matthew (2015), p 336.
52. Matthew (2015).
53. Bosworth (1988); Heckel (2008).
54. Arr. *Anab.* 2.10.5–6; Polyb. 12.22.
55. Matthew (2015), pp 194–6.
56. Matthew (2015), pp 196.
57. Matthew (2015), pp 196.
58. Curt. 3.11.5. Trans. Rolfe (modified slightly).
59. Matthew (2015), pp 195–6.
60. Lendon (2005), p 132.
61. Plut. *Aem.* 19.1–2.
62. Culham (1989).
63. Keegan (1987).
64. See Wheeler (2007) and Heckel (2008), pp 27–8.
65. Curt. 3.10.1.
66. Diod. Sic. 17.33.4; Matthew (2015), p 350.
67. Curt. 3.10.2–3. See too Diod. 17.33.4.
68. Curt. 3.11.1–2; Arr. *Anab.* 2.9.1.

69. See Wheeler (2007) and Heckel (2008), pp 27–8).
70. Heckel (2008), p. 61; Strauss (2012), p 77.
71. Arr. *Anab.* 2.10.3.
72. Curt. 3.11.7.
73. Diod. Sic. 17.33.5; Curt. 3.15.1–2.
74. Wrightson (2019).
75. Heckel (2008), p 64; Worthington (2017), p 531; Wrightson (2019).
76. Worthington (2017), pp 532–3.
77. Wrightson (2019), p 21.
78. Wrightson (2019), p 21.
79. Xen. *On Horsemanship* 3.12.
80. For all this, see Sears and Willekes (2016).
81. This evidence was highlighted by Sears and Willekes (2016), who drew
    on the fascinating research of Liston (2020), which is now published.
82. Liston (2020).
83. Strauss (2012), p 77; Sears and Willekes (2016). p 1027.
84. Arr. *Anab.* 2.12.1.
85. Lendon (2005), p 128; Worthington (2017), p 533.

Chapter 3: The Battle of Cannae (216 BC)

1. Smith (2007).
2. Levene (2010).
3. To see an excellent introduction and overview of the discipline, with a
   special emphasis on Greek warfare, check out her webinar listed here:
   https://www.wolfson.cam.ac.uk/about-wolfson/events/wolfson-ancient-
   warfare-wednesdays.
4. Ball (2016).
5. Ball (2016), p 37.
6. Polyb. 1.59–61.
7. Tusa and Royal (2012).
8. Bellón et al. (2016).
9. See Bellón Ruiz et al. (2017).
10. Polyb. 6.20.8–9.
11. Polyb. 3.106–118, Livy 22.44–52.
12. See Celsus, *Medicine* 7.5.
13. App. *Hann* 22.
14. Livy 25.12.5–6.
15. On skirmishing in Roman combat, see Anders (2015).
16. Hoyos (2007), p 70.
17. Culham (1989); Eckstein (2005).
18. Smith (2015), p 47.
19. Polyb. 3.108.6.
20. Asclepiodotus, *Tac.* 14.6; Xen. *Mem.* 3.19. See too Goldsworthy (1996),
    p 178.

21. See Lendon (2005).
22. Polyb. 3.114.6; Livy 22.45.
23. On the general course of ancient descriptions of battle see Lendon (2017a, 2017b).
24. For a new collection of essays that gets into some of the ins and outs of a wide range of military manuals, see Chlup and Whately (2020).
25. Polyb. 3.108–109, 111.
26. Livy 22.43. trans. Yardley.
27. Polyb. 3.108.9.
28. Livy 22.49.
29. Reid and Nicholson (2019).
30. To get a sense of this, see the following video: https://www.youtube.com/watch?v=7vJBKfQFD8I.
31. Polyb. 2.24.
32. Polyb. 3.109–110 (Paullus); 111–112 (Hannibal).
33. This famous and often-cited episode in Apuleius reads as follows (9.39ff.): 'But our return was not free from trouble. For we encountered a tall legionary soldier, as his dress and appearance indicated, who arrogantly and abusively demanded where he (the gardener) was taking the unladen ass. But my master, who was still rather perplexed, and ignorant of Latin, passed on without saying anything. The soldier, unable to contain his usual insolence and outraged at his silence as if it were an insult, struck him with the vine-wood staff he was holding and shoved him off my back. Then the gardener replied humbly that he could not make out what he had said because he did not understand his language. Then the soldier interjected in Greek: "Where are you taking this ass?"' [trans. Campbell].
34. Livy 5.37.8, 38.17.3; Polyb. 2.29.6; Tac. *Agr.* 33.
35. Livy 21.46.6. For more on this example and all the others, see Gersbach (2020), on which I draw heavily.
36. Livy 22.4.7, trans. Roberts.
37. Livy 30.34.1.
38. Polyb. 15.12, trans. Shuckburgh. See too Whately (2017a), p 69.
39. Dion. Hal. 8.84.
40. Plut. *Sul.* 14.
41. Cass. Dio 47.42; Joseph. *BJ.* 3.259.
42. Amm. Marc. 16.12.43; Veg. *Mil.* 3.18.9–10.
43. Vincent 2015a: 669.
44. Polyb. 14.3; Vincent 2015a: 670.
45. Livy 5.47.7; Vincent 2015a: 670.
46. Movement: Livy 2.59.6, Luc. 2.687–691; start of battle: Caes. *BCiv.* 3.90.3, Luc. 6.129–130, Polyb. 8.30.7; retreat: Caes. *BGall* 7.47, Polyb 15.14.3; Vincent (2015a), p 670.
47. Vincent (2015b), p 1020.

48. Some discussion in Sabin (2000, 2007); Zhmodikov (2000); Taylor (2014); and Roselaar (2015).
49. Koon (2011), p 80; Roselaar (2015).
50. Polyb. 3.115.3.
51. Polyb 3.116.10; Livy 22.48.
52. Koon (2011), p 83.
53. Livy 22.47.
54. Polyb. 3.116.4.
55. Polyb. 3.116.11–13.
56. Polyb. 3.116.11–13.
57. Livy 22.49.
58. Smith (2015), p 73.
59. Smith (2015), p 70.
60. Smith (2015), p 74.
61. Livy 22.49; Polyb. 3.117.2–4.
62. Smith (2015), p 82–3.
63. Fronda (2010).
64. Livy 27.19.
65. Smith (2015), p 106.
66. Hanson (1989), pp 126–31; Keegan (1976), pp 114–15, 183–4.
67. Tac. *Ann.* 1.65, *Hist.* 4.29; Goldsworthy (1996), pp 261–2.
68. I owe these facts to Dr Chris Whately, MD, FRCS (personal communication). See too James (2010).
69. Livy 22.51, trans. Roberts.
70. Livy 22.44, 49.
71. Livy 22.1.
72. Livy 22.6.
73. Livy 22.49.
74. Livy 22.51, trans. Roberts.
75. Livy 26.48.
76. Polyb. 10.14.14–15.
77. Polyb. 10.15.9.

Chapter 4: The Sieges of Jerusalem and Masada (66–74 CE)

1. The most detailed, recent, history of the Jewish War is Mason's (2016), which treats the bulk of the sources for the war, Josephus especially, in great detail. The material evidence is, to some degree, undervalued, but that shouldn't detract from the overall importance of his account.
2. For Josephus and the Jewish War, see Mason (2016), p 60–137.
3. Syon (2002); Reid and Nicholson (2019), p 474.
4. For a brief account of the war, see Campbell (2017).
5. Jos. *BJ.* 7.132.
6. For a good, and eminently readable, account of the siege of Jerusalem, see Levithan (2013), pp 142–69.

7. Tac. *Hist.*, 5.512.
8. Jos. *BJ* 6.193–198.
9. Spiciarich, Gadot, and Sapir-Hun (2017).
10. See Mason (2016), pp 118–21).
11. It's worth noting that the attacking soldiers might suffer in their own way. Mason (2016), p 181, for example, highlights the damage disease could cause to the besieging army.
12. Jos. *BJ.* 6.201–214, trans. Hammond.
13. Jos. *BJ* 6.420.
14. The account of Masada draws heavily from Magness' (2019) excellent new book.
15. See Magness (2019), pp 59–69).
16. Jos. *BJ* 7.252.
17. This summary is based on Levithan (2013) and Sidebottom (2017).
18. On the vast array of Roman siege works (in general – not here in particular), see Davies (2006).
19. Magness (2019), p 7–16.
20. Magness (2019), p 9–10.
21. On ancient artillery, see Marsden (1971).
22. On the military equipment from Masada, see Stiebel and Magness (2007).
23. Jos. *BJ.* 6.33ff.
24. Magness (2019), pp 12–16.
25. Magness (2019), pp 39–46.
26. Jos. *BJ.* 7.277–278.
27. Jos. *BJ.* 7.288.
28. Jos. *BJ.* 7.291.
29. Jos. *BJ.* 7.295–297.
30. Magness (2019), pp 168–9.
31. See Kirlev and Simchoni (2007). Their report is filled with images of the sorts of critters found at Masada.
32. Kirlev and Simchoni (2007), p 140.
33. Kirlev and Simchoni (2007), p 140.
34. Kirlev and Simchoni (2007), p 141–58.
35. Magness (2019), pp 183–5.
36. Jos, *BJ* 7.389–401, trans. Thackeray.
37. For more on Roman insurgencies, see Howe and Brice (2016).
38. For a fantastic and readable account of this archive and its value, see Esler (2017).
39. And in this, it reminds me of those wonderful, if haunting, Fayum portraits from Egypt.

Chapter 5: The Battle of Strasbourg (357 CE)

1. Blockley (1977); Kagan (2006); Ross (2016).
2. Some good accounts of the fourth century (CE) military include Elton (1996), Nicasie (1998), and Syvänne (2018).
3. See Matthews (1989).
4. See Kagan (2006).
5. Amm. Marc. 16.2.
6. Amm. Marc. 16.3.
7. Amm. Marc. 16.3.
8. Amm. Marc. 16.11.
9. Drinkwater (2007).
10. Amm. Marc. 16.12.7.
11. Amm. Marc. 16.12.19.
12. Amm. Marc. 16.21.1. A millennium if we're counting from Homer (around 700 BCE), a millennium and a half if we're counting from the supposed date of the war (around 1184 BCE).
13. Amm. Marc. 16.12.14, 27.
14. Amm. Marc. 15.12.2–7, 16.12.37ff.
15. Amm. Marc. 16.12. 43, 49.
16. Amm. Marc. 16.12.1.
17. Amm. Marc. 16.12.7.
18. Amm. Marc. 16.12.39.
19. Amm. Marc. 16.12.13.
20. Amm. Marc. 16.12.36.
21. Keegan (1976); Kagan (2006); Lenski (2007); Ross (2016).
22. See Ross (2014), for instance.
23. This literary dimension to Ammianus' and others' writing shouldn't diminish their value as sources for exploring the senses in ancient accounts of combat. For one thing, it means that contemporaries recognized the value of the senses in helping them make sense of the world. It also means we can expect more of the sorts of material that is essential to looking into this issue in more depth than we otherwise could. Finally, I'll add that there needn't be a discrepancy between literary tendencies and the historicity of sensory aspects in some writing. At least, I don't see it that way.
24. Amm. Marc. 16.12.8.
25. Amm. Marc. 16.12.9–12.
26. Amm. Marc. 16.12.18.
27. Amm. Marc. 16.12.29.
28. Amm. Marc. 16.12.34.
29. Amm. Marc. 16.12.43.
30. Amm. Marc. 31.7.11.
31. Tac. Germ. 3.

32. Amm. Marc. 14.10.14.
33. Amm. Marc. 15.2.1.
34. MacMullen (1964), p 445. Amm. Marc. 14.7.21, 15.2.1, 16.8.11, 20.5.2, 26.4.5, 28.1.14, 29.1.14, 31.13.1.
35. Amm. Marc. 18.4.1, 19.6.9, 19.7.3, 20.7.6, 20.11.8, 21.12.12, etc.
36. Den Boeft et al. (2002), p 120.
37. Amm. Marc. 19.11.15.
38. Amm. Marc. 31.7.10.
39. For a concise overview of the peculiarities of these and other instruments see Coulston (2015), pp 670–71.
40. Amm. Marc. 21.12.5.
41. Wille (1967), p 101; Den Boeft et al. (2002), p 120.
42. MacMullen (1964), p 83. CIL 3.10501; Fronto. PH. 2.209; REG 68: 276.
43. Amm. Marc. 16.12.46.
44. Amm. Marc. 16.12.52.
45. Amm. Marc. 16.12.46.
46. Amm. Marc. 16.12.53.
47. Amm. Marc 16.12.53.
48. Amm. Marc 16.12.52.
49. Amm. Marc 16.12.53.
50. Amm. Marc. 16.12.37.
51. Amm. Marc. 16.12.20.
52. Janniard (2011).
53. Amm. Marc. 16.12.44.
54. Amm. Marc. 16.12.22.
55. Amm. Marc. 16.12.52.
56. Amm. Marc. 16.12.54.
57. Amm. Marc. 16.12.53.
58. Amm Marc. 16.12.53.
59. Amm. Marc. 16.12.53.
60. Amm. Marc. 16.12.50.
61. Amm. Marc. 16.12.48.
62. Amm. Marc. 16.12.47.
63. Caes. *BG* 2.30.
64. For a good survey of this as it pertains to Roman populations, see Gowland and Walther (2018).
65. See Killgrove (2018).
66. See Giannecchini and Moggi-Cecchi (2008).
67. See Koepke and Baten (2005).
68. King (1999).
69. Toplyn (2006).
70. Crawford (2006).

71. On the earlier conditions and character of Roman military communities, see Allison (2013).
72. For a detailed study of rivers and Rome, see Campbell (2012).
73. Campbell (2012), p 194.
74. See the discussion in Campbell (2012), p 162.
75. Campbell (2012), p 163.
76. Caes. *BG.* 4.17.
77. Amm Marc. 16.1.5, trans. Rolfe.
78. Amm Marc. 16.10.6.
79. Amm Marc. 16.11.8–9, trans. Rolfe.
80. Campbell (2012), p 281.
81. Amm Marc. 16.12.11.
82. Amm Marc. 16.12.15.
83. Amm Marc. 16.12.19.
84. Amm Marc. 16.12.54.
85. Amm Marc. 16.12.55–56.
86. Amm Marc. 16.12.57.
87. Amm Marc. 16.12.57, trans. Rolfe.
88. Amm Marc. 16.12.58–59.
89. Amm Marc. 16.12.58–59, trans. Rolfe.
90. Amm Marc. 16.12.62.

Chapter 6: The Siege of Edessa (544 CE)
1. Standard accounts include Cameron (1985) and Kaldellis (2004). More recently, on more specifically military things, see Sarantis (2016); Stewart (2016); Whately (2016); and Parnell (2017). See too Stewart (2020). For an eclectic range of papers on Procopius, see Lillington-Martin and Turquois (2017) and Greatrex and Janniard (2018). For a readable overview of war in the age of Justinian, see Heather (2018). For the Romano-Persian war that preceded this one (involving Edessa), see Greatrex (1998).
2. For differing interpretations of the *Secret History*, see Brubaker (2004) and Börm (2015).
3. For our sources for war in late antiquity, see Whately (2013).
4. See Treadgold (2007) for an overview of early Byzantine historians.
5. See Greatrex (1998).
6. On the fortifications of the equally impressive site of Resafa, see Hof (2020).
7. On late antique walls and fortifications in general, see Johnson (1983).
8. See Jacobs (2013).
9. Procop. *Wars* 2.26.14.
10. Procopius says as much in his description of Edessa in the *Buildings* 2.7.8.
11. Procop. *Build.* 2.7.2–16; SH. 18.38.

12. Procop. *Wars* 2.26.11.
13. For some other conjectures, see Palmer (2000), pp 128–9).
14. Procop. *Wars* 2.26.25.
15. Procop. *Wars* 2.26.26.
16. Procop. *Wars* 2.26.28.
17. Procop. *Wars* 8.11.36.
18. Procop. *Wars* 2.27.19.
19. Procop. *Wars* 2.26.23.
20. Procop. *Wars* 2.26.29–30.
21. Procop. *Wars* 2.27.1.
22. Procop. *Wars* 2.27.2.
23. Procop. *Wars* 2.27.3.
24. Amm. Marc. 19.8.3–4., trans. Rolfe.
25. For the most plausible account of what transpired in the tower, see James (2011). For a detailed discussion of the military at Dura, see James' book (2019). Baird's book, on housing at Dura (2014), also gets into the military presence; for a concise introduction to the city, see her short book (2018).
26. On the military equipment see James (2004).
27. Procop. *Wars* 2.27.4, trans. Kaldellis.
28. Procop. *Wars* 2.27.7–8.
29. Procop. *Wars* 2.27.11–14.
30. Procop. *Wars* 2.27.15.
31. Evag. *EH* 4.27.
32. Euseb. *EH* 1.13.
33. Procop. *Wars* 2.12.
34. Evagrius relates the story at *EH* 4.27.
35. Evag. *EH* 4.27, trans. Whitby.
36. See Whately (2016), pp 44–5.
37. Whately (2016), pp 101–5.
38. Procop. *Wars* 2.26.2–4.
39. Procop. *Wars* 2.12.32, 2.13.3.
40. Procop. *Wars* 2.26.12.
41. Procop. *Wars* 2.26.5.
42. Procop. *Build.* 2.7.2–9; Palmer (2000).
43. Mayor (2015).
44. Again, on this, see Mayor (2015).
45. See Greene (2015), for instance.
46. Procop. *Wars* 2.27.32.
47. Procop. *Wars* 2.27.35.
48. Pseudo-Joshua Stylites 60.288, trans. Trombley and Watt.
49. Procop. *Wars* 1.7.19, trans. Kaldellis. On women and sieges in Procopius, see Whately (2016), pp 73–4.

50. Procop. *Wars* 2.27.36.
51. Procop. *Wars* 1.21.5, 5.5.3, 5.16.2.
52. On the complexities of Procopius' characterization of Bessas, see Whately (2017b).
53. Parnell (2017), p 86.
54. Procop. *Wars* 7.17.9–21, trans. Kaldellis (slightly modified).
55. Procop. *Wars* 7.19.14, trans. Kaldellis (slightly modified).
56. Procop. *Wars* 8.14.35.
57. Procop. *Wars* 8.14.37.

Bibliography and Further Reading

By no means is the bibliography provided here and in each chapter meant to be exhaustive and definitive. Hopefully, it is at least representative of much of the good work being done on war and warfare in the ancient Mediterranean. Given the intended audience of this book (largely Anglophone), nearly all of the works cited are in English. But readers should be aware that quite a lot of important research is published in other languages, like French, German, Italian, Spanish, and more. Finally, those looking for a readable introduction to Greek warfare should seek out Sears (2019) and also Sears and Butera (2019). For what I hope is a comparable Roman option, see Whately (2020). For sensory history and warfare, read Smith (2015), as I noted at the beginning, the inspiration for this small book.

Allison, P. (2013), *People and Spaces in Roman Military Bases* (Cambridge).

Anders, A. (2015), 'The Face of Roman Skirmishing', *Historia* 64, pp 263–300.

Anson, E. (2010), 'The General's Pre-Battle Exhortation in Graeco-Roman Warfare', *G & R* 57, pp 304–18.

Baird, J. (2014), *The Inner Lives of Ancient Houses: An Archaeology of Dura-Europos* (London).

Baird, J. (2018), *Dura Europos* (London).

Ball, J. (2016), *Collecting the Field: A Methodological Reassessment of Greek and Roman Battlefield Archaeology*, PhD thesis, University of Liverpool.

Bellón, J. P.; Rueda, C.; Lechuga M. A.; and María Isabel Moreno (2016). 'An archaeological analysis of a battlefield of the Second Punic War: the camps of the battle of Baecula', *JRA* 29, pp 73–104.

Bellón Ruiz, J. P.; Rueda Galán, C.; Lechuga Chica, M. A.; Rodríguez, R. A.; and Molinos, M. M. (2017), 'Archaeological methodology applied to the analysis of battlefields and military camps of the Second Punic War: Baecula', *Quarternary International* 435, pp 81–97.

Blockley, R. C. (1977), 'Ammianus Marcellinus on the Battle of Strasburg: Art and Analysis in the History', *Phoenix* 31, pp. 218–31.

Börm, H. (2015), 'Procopius, his Predecessors, and the Genesis of the Anecdota: Antimonarchic discourse in Late Antique Historiography', in H. Börm (ed), *Antimonarchic Discourse in Antiquity* (Stuttgart), pp 305–46.

Bosworth, A. B. (1988), *Conquest and Empire: the Reign of Alexander the Great* (Cambridge).

Bradley, M. (ed) (2014), *Smell and the Ancient Senses* (London).

Brice, L. (2011), 'Philip II, Alexander the Great, and the Question of a Macedonian "Revolution in Military Affairs (RMA)"', *Ancient World* 42, pp 137–47.

Brubaker, L. (2004), 'Sex, Lies, and Textuality: The Secret History of Prokopios and the Rhetoric of Gender in Sixth-Century Byzantium', in L. Brubaker and J. M. H. Smith (eds), *Gender in the Early Medieval World, East and West, 300–900* (Cambridge), pp 83–101.

Bugh, G. R. (2006), 'Hellenistic Military Developments', in G. R. Bugh (ed), *The Cambridge Companion to the Hellenistic World* (Cambridge), pp 265–94.

Butler, S. and A. Purves (eds) (2014), *Synaesthesia and the Ancient Senses* (London)

Cameron, A. (1985), *Procopius and the Sixth Century* (London)

Campbell, B. (2012), *Rivers and the Power of Ancient Rome* (Chapel Hill).

Campbell, B. (2017), 'The Jewish Revolt, 66', in Whitby, M. and H. Sidebottom (eds), *The Encyclopedia of Ancient Battles* (Malden, MA), pp 1004–10.

Chlup, J., and C. Whately (eds) (2020), *Greek and Roman Military Manuals: Genre and History* (London).

Clunn, T. (2005), *The Quest for Rome's Lost Legions: Discovering the Varus Battlefield* (New York).

Coulston, J. C. (2015), 'Music: Principate', in Y. Le Bohec (ed), *Encyclopedia of the Roman Army* (Malden, MA), pp 670–71.

Crawford, P. (2006), 'The Plant Remains', in S. T. Parker (ed), *The Roman Frontier in Central Jordan: Final report on the Limes Arabicus Project, 1980–1989* (Washington, DC), pp 453–61.

Culham, P. (1989), 'Chance, command, and chaos in ancient military engagements', *World Futures*, 27, pp 191–205.

Cuomo, S. (2007), *Technology and Culture in Greek and Roman Antiquity* (Cambridge).

Daly, G. (2000), *Cannae: the Experience of Battle in the Second Punic War* (London).

Davies, G. (2006) *Roman Siege Works* (Cheltenham).

Den Boeft, J.; Drijvers, J.; den Hengst, D.; and Teitler H. (2002), *Philological and historical commentary on Ammianus Marcellinus XXIV* (Leiden).

Echeverría, F. (2011), 'Taktikè technè. The neglected element in classical hoplite battles', *Ancient Society* 41, pp 45–82.

Echeverría, F. (2012), 'Hoplite and Phalanx in Archaic and Classical Greece: A Reassessment', *CP* 107, pp 291–318.

Eckstein, A., (2005), 'Bellicosity and Anarchy: Soldiers, Warriors, and Combat in Antiquity', *International History Review* 27, pp 481–97.

Esler, P. (2017), *Babatha's Orchard. The Yadin Papyri and an Ancient Jewish Family Tale Retold* (Oxford).

Flower, M. (2012), *Xenophon's Anabasis or the Expedition of Cyrus* (New York).

Fox, R. L. (ed) (2004), *The Long March: Xenophon and the Ten Thousand* (New Haven).

Fronda, M. (2010), *Between Rome and Carthage: Southern Italy during the Second Punic War* (Cambridge).

Gersbach, J. (2020), *The War Cry in the Ancient Mediterranean World* (Cambridge).

Giannecchini, M. and J. Moggi-Cecchi (2008) 'Stature in Archaeological Samples from Central Italy: Methodological Issues and Diachronic Changes', *American Journal of Physical Anthropology* 135, pp 284–92.

Goldsworthy, A. (1996), *The Roman Army at War 100 BC to AD 200* (Oxford).

Gowland, R. and L. Walther (2018), 'Human Growth and Stature', in W. Scheidel (ed), *The Science of Roman History* (Princeton), pp 174–204.

Greatrex, G (1998), *Rome and Persia at War, AD 502–532* (Leeds).

Greatrex, G. and S. Janniard (eds) (2018), *The World of Procopius/Le Monde de Procope* (Paris).

Greene, E. (2015), 'Conubium cum uxoribus: wives and children in the Roman military diplomas', *JRA* 28, pp 125–59.

Greenwood, E. (2006) *Thucydides and the Shaping of History* (London).

Hamilakis, Y. (2013) *Archaeology of the Senses: Human Experience, Memory, and Affect* (Cambridge).

Hansen, M. (1993), 'The Battle Exhortation in Ancient Historiography: Fact or Fiction?' *Historia* 42, pp 161–180.

Hansen, M. (2001), 'The Little Grey Horse: Henry V's Speech at Agincourt and the Battle Exhortation in Ancient Historiography', *C & M* 52, pp 95–116.

Hanson, V. D., (1989), *The Western Way of War* (Berkeley)

Heather, P. (2018), *Rome Resurgent* (Oxford).

Heckel, W. (2008), *The Conquests of Alexander the Great* (Cambridge).

Hof, C. (2020), *Resafa 9,1. Resafa-Sergiupolis/Rusafat Hisham* (Wiesbaden).

Howe, T. and L. Brice (ed) (2016), *Brill's Companion to Insurgency and Terrorism in the Ancient Mediterranean World* (Leiden).

Hoyos, D. (2007), 'The Age of Overseas Expansion (264–146 BCE)', in P. Erdkamp (ed.), *A Companion to the Roman Army* (Malden, MA), pp 63–79.

Hunt, P. 2007, 'Military Forces [Archaic and Classical Greece]', in Sabin, P., Van Wees, H. and M. Whitby (eds), *The Cambridge History of Greek and Roman Warfare Volume I: Greece, the Hellenistic World and the rise of Rome* (Cambridge, pp 108–46).

Jacobs, I. (2013) *Aesthetic Maintenance of Civic Space* (Leuven).

James, S. (2004) *The Excavations at Dura-Europos conducted by Yale University and the French Academy of Inscriptions and Letters 1928 to 1937. Final Report VII: The Arms and Armour and other Military Equipment* (Oxford).

James, S. (2010), 'The Point of the Sword: what Roman-era weapons could do to bodies – and why they often didn't', in A. W. Busch and H. J. Schalles (eds.), *Waffen in Aktion. Akten der 16. Internationalen Roman Military Equipment Conference (ROMEC), Xantaner Berichte 16* (Xanten) pp 41–54.

James, S. (2011), 'Stratagems, Combat, and "Chemical Warfare" in the Siege Mines of Dura-Europos', *AJA* 115, pp 69–101.

James, S. (2019), *The Roman Military Bases at Dura Europos* (Oxford).

Janniard, S. (2011), *Les Transformations de l'Armée Romano-Byzantine (IIIe – VIe Siècles apr. J.-C.): Le Paradigme de la Bataille Rangée*, Unpublished PhD thesis, L'Atelier du Centre de Recherches Historiques.

Johnson, S. (1983), *Late Roman Fortifications* (London).

Kagan, K. (2006), *The Eye of Command* (Ann Arbor).

Kaldellis, A. (2004), *Procopius of Caesarea: Tryanny, History, and Philosophy at the End of Antiquity* (Philadelphia).

Keegan, J. (1976), *The Face of Battle* (London).

Keegan, J. (1987), *The Mask of Command* (London).

Killgrove, K., 'Using Skeletal Remains as a Proxy for Roman Lifestyles: the potential and problems with osteological reconstructions of health, diet and stature in Imperial Rome', in Erdkamp, P. and C. Holleran (eds), *The Routledge Handbook of Diet and Nutrition in the Roman World* (London, pp 245–258).

Kislev, M. and O. Simchoni (2007) , 'Hygiene and Insect Damage of Crops and Food at Masada', in Aviram, J.; Foerster, G.; Netzer, E.; and G. Stiebel (eds), *Masada VIII. The Yigael Yadin Excavations 1963–1965* (Jerusalem), pp 133–170.

Koepke, N., and J. Baten (2005), 'The Biological Standard of Living in Europe during the Last Two Millenia', *European Review of Economic History* 9, pp 61–95.

Konijendijk, R. (2018), *Classical Greek Tactics: A Cultural History* (Leiden).

Koon, S. (2011), 'Phalanx and Legion: The "Face" of Punic War Battle', in D. Hoyos (ed), *A Companion to the Punic Wars* (Malden, MA), pp 77–94.

Krentz, P. (1985), 'The Nature of Hoplite Battle', *CA* 4, pp 50–61.

Krentz, P. (2010), *The Battle of Marathon* (New Haven).

Lazenby, J. (1991), 'The Killing Zone', in V. D. Hanson (ed), *Hoplites: the Classical Greek Battle Experience* (London), pp 87–109.

Lee, J. (2007). *A Greek Army on the March* (Cambridge).

Lendon, J. E. (2005), *Soldiers and Ghosts* (New Haven).

Lendon, J. E. (2017a), 'Battle Description in the Ancient Historians, Part I: Structure, Array, and Fighting', *G & R* 64, pp 39–64.

Lendon, J. E. (2017b), 'Battle Description in the Ancient Historians, Part II: Speeches, Results, and Sea Battles', *G & R* 64, pp 145–167.

Lenski, N. (2007), 'Two Sieges of Amida (AD 359 and 502–503) and the Experience of Combat in the Late Roman East', in A. S. Lewin and P. Pellegrini (eds), *The Late Roman Army in the Near East from Diocletian to the Arab Conquest* (Oxford, 219–236).

Lenski (2007), 'Two Sieges of Amida (AD 359 and 502–503) and the Experience of Combat in the Late Roman Near East', in Lewin and Pellegrini (2007), pp 219–36.

Levene, D. S. (2010), *Livy on the Hannibalic War* (Oxford).

Levithan, J. (2013), *Roman Siege Warfare* (Ann Arbor).

Lillington, C. and E. Turquois, (eds) (2017) *Procopius of Caesarea: Literary and Historical Interpretations* (London).

Liston, M. (2020), 'Skeletal Evidence for the Impact of Battle on Soldiers and Non-Combatants', in L. Brice (ed), *New Approaches to Greco-Roman Warfare* (Malden, MA), pp 81–94.

MacMullen, R. (1963), *Soldier and Civilian in the Later Roman Empire*, (Cambridge, MA).

MacMullen, R. (1964), 'Some Images in Ammianus Marcellinus', *Art Bulletin* 46, pp 435–55.

Magness, J. (2019), *Masada: From Jewish Revolt to Modern Myth* (Princeton).

Manning, S. (2021), *Armed Force in the Teispid-Achaemenid Empire* (Stuttgart).

Marsden, E. W. (1971), *Greek and Roman Artillery* (Oxford).

Matthew, C. (2015), *An Invincible Beast: Understanding the Hellenistic Pike Phalanx in Action* (Barnsley)

Matthews, J. (1989), *The Roman Empire of Ammianus* (London).

Mayor, A. (2015), *The Amazons: Lives and Legends of Warrior Women Across the Ancient World* (Princeton).

Moore, R. (2013), 'Generalship: Leadership and Command', in B. Campbell and L. Tritle (eds), *The Oxford Handbook of Warfare in the Classical World* (Oxford), pp 457–73.

Murdoch, A. (2008), *Rome's Greatest Defeat*, (Gloucester).

Palmer, A. (2000), 'Procopius and Edessa', *AntTard* 8, pp 127–36.

Parnell, D. (2017), *Justinian's Men* (London).

Pritchett, W. K. (1994), 'The General's Exhortations', in *Essays in Greek History* (Amsterdam), pp 111–44.

Pritchett, W. K. (2002), *Ancient Greek Battle Speeches and a Palfrey* (Amsterdam).

Reid, J. and A. Nicholson (2019), 'Burnswark Hill: the opening shot of the Antonine reconquest of Scotland?', *JRA* 32, pp 459–77.

Rop, J. (2019) *Greek military service in the ancient Near East, 401–330 BCE* (Cambridge).

Roselaar, S. (2015), 'Battle formation in the Roman Republic: parade show or practical purpose?', *Revue Internationale d'histoire militaire ancienne* 2, pp 23–53.

Ross, A. (2014), 'Constantius and the Sieges of Amida and Nisibis: Ammianus' Relationship with Julian's "Panegyrics"', *Acta Classica* 57, pp 127–54.

Ross, A. (2016), *Ammianus' Julian: Narrative and Genre in the Res Gestae* (Oxford).

Rutherford, I. (2004), '"Lovers of Sights and Sounds": Perception and Its Enemies in Greco-Roman Thought and Culture', in T. Fischer-Seidel, S. Peters, and A. Potts (eds), *Perception and the Senses* (Tubingen), pp 67–82.

Sabin, P. (2000), 'The Face of Roman Battle', *JRS* 90, pp 1–17.

Sabin, P. (2007), *Lost Battles: Reconstructing the Great Clashes of the Ancient World* (London).

Sarantis, A. (2016), *Justinian's Balkan Wars* (Cambridge).

Schwartz, A. (2009), *Reinstating the Hoplite. Arms, Armour and Phalanx Fighting in Archaic and Classical Greece* (Stuttgart).

Schwartz, A. (2013), 'Large Weapons, Small Greeks: The Practical Limitations of Hoplite Weapons and Equipment', in Kagan, D. and G. Viggiano (eds), *Men of Bronze: Hoplite Warfare in Ancient Greece* (Princeton), pp 157–75.

Sears, M. (2019), *Understanding Greek Warfare* (London).

Sears, M. and J. Butera (2019), *Battles and Battlefields of Ancient Greece* (Barnsley).

Sears, M. and C. Willekes (2016), 'Alexander's Cavalry Charge at Chaeronea, 338 BCE', *JMH* 80, pp 1017–35.

Sekunda, N. (2007), 'Military Forces [The Hellenistic World and the Roman Republic]', in Sabin, P., Whitby, M., and H. Van Wees (eds), *The Cambridge History of Greek and Roman Warfare Volume I: Greece, the Hellenistic World and the rise of Rome* (Cambridge), pp 325–57.

Sidebottom, H. (2017), 'Ancient Siege Warfare, 700 BC–AD 645', in Whitby, M. and H. Sidebottom (eds), *The Encyclopedia of Ancient Battles*, pp 42–82.

Smith, M. (2003), 'Making Sense of Social History', *Journal of Social History* 37, pp 165–86.

Smith, M. (2007), 'Producing Sense, Consuming Sense, Making Sense: Perils and Prospects for Sensory History', *Journal of Social History* 40, pp 841–58.

Smith, M. (2010), *Sensory History* London.

Smith, M. (2015), *The Smell of Battle, the Taste of Siege* (New York).

Snodgrass, A. (2013), 'Setting the Frame Chronologically', in D. Kagan and G. Viggiano (eds), *Men of Bronze: Hoplite Warfare in Ancient Greece* (Princeton), pp 85–94.

Spiciarich, A., Y. Gadot and S. L. apir-Hun (2017), 'The Faunal Evidence from Early Roman Jerusalem: The People behind the Garbage', *Tel Aviv* 44, pp 98–117.

Squire, M. (ed) (2016a), *Sight and the Ancient Senses* (London).

Squire ,M. (2016b) 'Introductory reflections: Making sense of ancient sight', in Squire (2016a).

Stewart, M. (2016), *The Soldier's Life* (Leeds).

Stewart, M. (2020), *Masculinity, Identity, and Power Politics in the Age of Justinian* (Amsterdam).

Stiebel, G. and J. Magness (2007), 'The Military Equipment from Masada', in J. Aviram, G. Foerster, E. Netzer and G. Stiebel (eds), *Masada VIII. The Yigael Yadin Excavations 1963–1965* (Jerusalem), pp 1–94.

Strauss, B. (2006), *The Trojan War: A New History* (New York).

Strauss, B. (2012) *Masters of Command* (New York).

Stylianou, P. J. (2004), 'One Anabasis or Two?', in R. L. Fox (ed), *The Long March: Xenophon and the Ten Thousand* (New Haven), pp 68–96.

Synott, A. (1993), 'Puzzling Over the Senses: from Plato to Marx', in D. Howes (ed), *The Varieties of Sensory Experience: a Sourcebook in the Anthropology of the Senses* Toronto, pp 61–76.

Syon, D. (2002), 'Gamla – city of refuge', in A. M. Berlin and J. A. Overman (eds), *The First Jewish Revolt: archaeology, history and ideology* (London), pp 134–53.

Taylor, M. (2014), 'Roman Infantry Tactics in the Mid-Republic: A Reassessment', *Historia* 63, pp 301–22.

Toplyn, M. (2006), 'Livestock and Limitanei: The Zooarchaeological Evidence', in S. T. Parker (ed), *The Roman Frontier in Central Jordan: Final report on the Limes Arabicus Project, 1980–1989* (Washington, DC), pp 463–507.

Treadgold, W. (2007), *The Early Byzantine Historians* (London).

Trundle, M. (2017), 'The Anabasis and the Ten Thousand, 401–399 BCE', in M. Whitby and H. Sidebottom (eds), *The Encyclopedia of Ancient Battles* (Malden, MA), pp 408–16.

Tusa, S. and J. Royal (2012), 'The landscape of the naval battle at the Egadi Islands (241 B.C.)', *JRA* 25, pp 7–48.

Van Wees, H. (1988), 'Kings in combat: battles and heroes in the Iliad', *CQ* 38, pp 1–24.

Van Wees, H. (1992), *Status Warriors: Violence and Society in Homer and History* (Amsterdam).

Van Wees, H. (1994), 'The Homeric way of war: the Iliad and the hoplite phalanx (I) and (II)', *G & R* 41, pp 1–18, 131–55.

Van Wees, H. (1996), 'Heroes, knights and nutters: warrior mentality in Homer', in A. B. Lloyd (ed), *Battle in Antiquity* (Swansea), pp 1–86.

Van Wees, H. (2004), *Greek Warfare: Myths and Realities* (London).

Varto, E. (forthcoming), 'Brotherhoods to Bodyguards: Competition, Cooperation, and the Phratry in Early Greek Warfare', in M. Hebblewhite and C. Whately (eds), *A Companion to Bodyguards in the Ancient Mediterranean World* (Leiden).

Vincent, A. (2015a), 'Music: Republic', in Y. Le Bohec (ed), *Encyclopedia of the Roman Army* (Malden, MA), pp 669–70.

Vincent, A. (2015b), 'Transmission of Orders: Republic', in Y. Le Bohec (ed), *Encyclopedia of the Roman Army* (Malden, MA), pp 1020.

Wells, P. (2003), *The Battle that Stopped Rome* (New York).

Whately, C. (2013), 'War in Late Antiquity: Secondary Works, Literary Sources and Material Evidence', in A. Sarantis and N. Christie (eds), *War and Warfare in Late Antiquity: Current Perspectives* (Leiden), pp 101–51.

Whately, C. (2016) *Battles and Generals: Combat, Culture, and Didacticism in Procopius' Wars* (Leiden).

Whately, C. (2017a), 'The War Cry: Ritualized Behaviour and Roman Identity in Ancient Warfare, 200 BC–AD 400', in A. Zuiderhoek and W. Vanacker (eds), *Imperial Identities in the Roman World* (London), pp 61–77.

Whately, C. (2017b), 'Procopius and the Characterization of Bessas: Where History Meets Historiography', in E. Turquois and C. Lillington-Martin (eds), *Procopius of Caesarea: Literary and Historical Interpretations* (London), pp 123–36.

Whately, C. (2020), *The Roman Military from Marius to Theodosius II* (Malden, MA).

Wheeler, E. (1991), 'The General as Hoplite', in V. D. Hanson (ed), *Hoplites: the Classical Greek Battle Experience* (London), pp 121–70.

Wheeler, E. (2001), 'Firepower: Missile Weapons and the "Face of Battle"', *Electrum* 5, pp 169–84.

Wheeler, E. (2007), 'Battle: A. Land Battles [Archaic and Classical Greece]', in P. Sabin, H Van Wees and M. Whitby (eds), *The Cambridge History of Greek and Roman Warfare Volume I: Greece, the Hellenistic World and the rise of Rome* (Cambridge), pp186–223.

Whitby, M. (2004), 'Xenophon's Ten Thousand as a Fighting Force', in R. L. Fox, (ed), *The Long March: Xenophon and the Ten Thousand* (New Haven), pp 215–42.

Wille, G. (1967), *Musica Romana* (Amsterdam).

Worthington, I. (2017), 'Campaigns of Alexander the Great, 336–323 BC', in M. Whitby and H. Sidebottom (eds), *The Encyclopedia of Ancient Battles* (Malden, MA), pp 503–73.

Wrightson, G. (2019), *Combined Arms Warfare in Ancient Greece* (London).

Zhmodikov, A. (2000), 'Roman Republican Heavy Infantrymen in Battle (IV–II Centuries B.C.)', *Historia* 49, pp 67–78.

Index